Celebrations

for Everyday and Special Occasions

Patty Sachs & Phyllis Cambria

Pascoe Publishing, Inc.
Rocklin, California

Cover and Interior Design by Knockout Books

Published in the United States of America by
Pascoe Publishing, Inc.
Rocklin, California
http://www.pascoepublishing.com

ISBN 1-929862-37-7

04 05 06   10 9 8 7 6 5 4 3 2

Printed in Hong Kong

Table of Contents

Introduction

Starting a new life together is fun! You'll share a lot over the coming years and some of the best times will undoubtedly take place in your kitchen. Cooking as a couple is an adventure and the right tools make it easy. Cuisinart® products are designed to let you do all the basics and to exercise your culinary creativity whenever the whim strikes. Our products will really make a difference in your life. They can handle everything from time-consuming food prep to toasting, brewing, mixing, blending, cooking, baking and broiling. Take a look inside at our innovative new products and recipes we've developed for you right in our own Cuisinart kitchens. And have fun!

Mary Rodgers

Chapter 1

The New Beginnings

When the whirlwind of pre-wedding parties, the ceremony, the reception and your honeymoon are behind you, chances are you may be feeling a little low because the excitement seems to have died down. But the truth is that this is just the beginning of a lifetime of festivities and entertaining for you and your spouse.

Now you have the opportunity to start a new set of memories through the entertaining you will do together. The parties and the occasions that you celebrate will take on new meaning as you make these plans as host and hostess and create these events and memories as a team.

Small celebrations to acknowledge significant events are the perfect time to bring together family and friends. Entertaining with dinner parties and supper clubs is an ideal format for good food and great company. You will create new and lasting memories and bring everyone closer together. Of course, there is a long list of typical occasions that always inspire us to celebrate at home, such as birthdays, anniversaries and holidays. Then there are the milestone events such as christenings, graduations, a Bris and pre-wedding parties, all of which are perfect for home entertaining.

Your newly acquired Cuisinart® appliances can be the beginning of your inspiration to entertain. These appliances will join you as "co-hosts" to make your hosting duties not only easier, but also a lot more fun.

So, if you haven't unpacked your beautiful Cuisinart® gifts yet, now is the time to find a prominent and easy-to-reach place for them in your cupboards, on open shelves, on your kitchen counter or on your kitchen island. You'll want to keep them all close because you'll be calling upon them often, not only for daily needs, but for their co-hosting duties as well.

Need some tips, hints and ideas before extending that first invitation? That's where this book, *Celebrations for Everyday and Special Occasions*, along with your team of Cuisinart® "co-hosts," comes in.

In this reader-friendly book, you will find clever and creative tips and tactics to help you earn praise from your guests as warm, thoughtful and natural hosts. You will also find a generous collection of kitchen tested and easily prepared recipes with excellent serving suggestions to enhance each occasion.

Celebrations for Everyday and Special Occasions gives you not only food and beverage recipes and ideas, but also a substantial amount of up-to-date information on invitations, decorations, table setting, etiquette and take-home favors to paint a complete party-giving picture.

However, not all parties have to be complicated events that require weeks of preparation. In fact, some of the best celebrations you'll create will be those occasions when you pull together a last minute gathering for your friends or a spur-of-the-moment get-together for a few family members.

As a matter of fact, one of your most treasured private celebration times might be just the two of you sipping a café latte and munching on just-baked cookies as you create a scrapbook of your wedding photos. In the quiet of your home, you can cuddle and laugh while remembering the romantic and unforgettable moments you recently shared, and dream of future special occasions. Can you think of a more meaningful celebration?

Want to know how to enhance your relationship with your new, extended family through entertaining? Along with building up a treasure trove of mutual memories with these folks, sincere flattery can be another step to bonding with family members. For example: fix your father-in-law's favorite dish, ask your new aunt for her famous potato salad recipe and cajole your mother-in-law into sharing her secrets for the perfect beef gravy. In turn, your spouse can ask your dad for his tips on carving the holiday turkey or coax your uncle into making his secret barbecue sauce at your next outdoor event. All of these are ways to become closer to your new relatives while building up a lifetime of traditions for future generations.

While special days such as holidays, birthdays and anniversaries are the best-known times to bring everyone together, it doesn't have to be a recognized occasion for you to want to commemorate it. Here are just a few of the fun accomplishments or occasions you might want to acknowledge with a spontaneous, and sometimes, same day celebration:

- Team victories
- Getting raises and promotions
- Closing escrow on your new home
- Announcing you're starting a family
- Opening a new business or starting a new job
- An improved report card for your child, step-child, niece or nephew
- A role in a community theatre production
- Christening a new car, boat or computer
- Televised sporting events or specials
- Movie nights at home
- Board game night
- After-theatre or post-dinner gatherings
- Harvesting a crop from your garden
- Making crafts for a holiday

Of course, there are dozens of reasons to celebrate. Watch for any reason to put together impromptu gatherings. You might pick a silly day to celebrate such as April 6th, which is North Pole Discovery Day, and make Eskimo pies with your ice cream maker. National Blueberry Muffin Day is on June 11th. Partner with your food processor and whip up a few batches of muffins and either invite your neighbors in for a spontaneous get-together, or deliver the muffins as a way to introduce yourself to new neighbors.

The second Thursday in October is National Dessert Day, so put your toaster oven into service to make a batch of brownies to bring to work. April 23rd, National Electric Mixer Day, is a great reason to whip up a party of your own design.

We know one very enthusiastic and creative hostess who held an impromptu gathering to celebrate her sparkling new hand mixer. All the guests, as instructed, came dressed in white to pay tribute to the honored appliance and, to keep the theme, brought gifts of cake mixes, frosting and other baking ingredients to the blanc bash.

Now, isn't that the best type of instantly inspired fun occasion?

And who said celebrations have to be limited to weekends or evenings? Think of the fun of getting the family together for a Saturday morning early bird breakfast that stars your Cuisinart® waffle maker doing its finest work.

The office gang will be truly energized during those late afternoon meetings once they've enjoyed a scrumptious cookie, created and baked in your own home.

How about a mid-week ice cream social to get your friends through to Friday, while they enjoy a TV special or a board game with your frosty refreshments? Just be sure to invite your guests into your kitchen to meet your ice cream/sorbet maker and your other Cuisinart® helpers.

When you make plans for any of these gatherings, whether they are small or large, to acknowledge or celebrate, you'll be truly happy to have your Cuisinart® appliances to assist you. You can count on a variety of specialty drinks mixed in your blender and delicious, hot hors d'oeuvres straight from your toaster oven, to be the hit of any cocktail gathering or get-together.

Then, imagine your guests' reaction to the aromatic fragrance of fresh ground and brewed coffee from your programmable coffee maker, mixed with the aroma of just-baked sweet rolls prepared with your hand mixer.

Added to the joy and ease of everyday cooking, all of these pleasurable experiences can be explored and shared as a couple. On the other hand, many of Cuisinart's® cook-without-looking appliances will give you more time to unwind as you and your partner exchange stories of the day. Relax in the knowledge that you can create delectable meals in minutes with Cuisinart's® state-of-the-art small kitchen appliances.

Best of all, studies show that getting together with loved ones to share special times is actually good for your mental, spiritual and physical health. So, don't just live your life, celebrate it...together! Keep the excitement of your wedding festivities with you happily ever after. It's good for you and all those that you love.

Chapter 2

Festive Fundamentals

First Things First

You've decided that you want to entertain or have a celebration. Great! With this step-by-step guide you will gain information and inspiration to host a get-together with the ease and style of a party pro.

Let's Party – What's the Occasion

- Formal celebrations like birthdays, anniversaries, a new business opening, etc.
- Casual celebrations like dinner with friends, supper clubs, backyard barbeques, etc.

Bank on It – Formal Party Budget

- Printed materials (invitations, menu cards, place cards)   3 percent
- Food and beverages, including labor, if any   40 percent
- Decorations (linens, balloons, centerpieces, banners)   15 percent
- Rental items (tables, chairs, dishes, glassware)   14 percent
- Entertainment and activities   20 percent
- Prizes, gifts and favors   3 percent
- Miscellaneous   5 percent

Please Join Us For...

Determine the time and type of party you would like to host:

- Breakfast
- Brunch

- Lunch
- Late afternoon tea or dessert gathering
- Picnic/Barbecue/Tailgate
- Cocktail reception
- Buffet or sit-down dinner
- Post-dinner cocktails or dessert gathering
- Late evening/post-event gathering for desserts and/or a "midnight" breakfast
- Dinner with friends, supper clubs

Pencil Us In

Aside from times suiting your schedule, there are some days and times that are better than others for parties, depending on your target guest list:

- Family get-togethers - Saturday or Sunday from brunch through early evening.
- Entertaining co-workers or clients - Tuesday through Thursday is best from 5:30 p.m. to 8 p.m. for cocktail events, or 6 p.m. to 9 p.m. for dinner events.
- Planned dinner parties - Friday or Saturday evenings.

Room For One More?

- Determine where you plan to entertain to determine the amount of guests you can accommodate for the type of party you will be hosting.
- Don't forget more unusual spaces such as terraces, porches, or a spruced-up garage. These can be ideal entertaining spaces.
- Limit the number of guests at a sit-down dinner party to the amount of people you can accommodate at one or two tables. Keep the second table close to and decorated comparably to the first for continuity. With two tables, be sure there is a gracious host sitting at each.
- Remember, even if you serve a buffet-style meal, you will require seating for all of your guests throughout your entertainment area. Only finger-food can be easily enjoyed while standing.

Guess Who's Coming to Dinner?

Once you have decided how many guests you want to have, create the guest list. Include:

- Family and friends of the guest(s) of honor at a birthday or anniversary festivity.
- Co-workers or clients when entertaining for business occasions.
- Work-mates, family and neighbors for holiday open houses or large-scale parties.
- Close friends for that casual dinner party.

Hosting Helper

At large parties, your varied guest list will easily mix when you, as their thoughtful hosts, have introduced "like-interest" guests to each other.

Overall, when given the choice, try to select guests who not only suit the occasion, but who also would enjoy each other's company.

To Theme or Not to Theme

A theme can add interest and excitement to even the most routine event and has the added bonus of helping you stretch your budget. For instance, on a hot dog and hamburger budget, themes such as "Country Fair," "The Wild West" or "Under the Big Top" would feature those foods perfectly. You can also stretch your budget with many Italian, Mexican, Asian and old-fashioned potluck cuisines.

For special tribute occasions, consider the interests, talents, heritage or hobbies of the guest(s) of honor to help you choose an appropriate theme.

No guest of honor? Then select a theme your guests will enjoy and which suits the party space. For example, if your home has an Early American design and décor, patriotic, historic, or country fair themes will suit your site. Of course you could host a high-tech, ultra-modern martini party but you would have to spend considerably more on your party decorations to adapt your space to that theme.

Then, simply add the specific theme details for all your party's elements, from the invitation to the party favors and everything in between.

Themes are not always necessary. In fact, for the casual get-together all a celebration needs are good friends, good food and good drinks.

Park It Here

If you do not have adequate parking, check with your neighbors to see what extra spaces they may let you use. If parking is still a problem, instruct guests to park at a nearby public parking lot and arrange for guests to be shuttled to your party site. For larger groups or in cold or foul weather you can have a few volunteers act as a valet.

Hosting Helper

Take special care in providing nearby or valet parking for elderly or handicapped guests.

Meals in Minutes

To cook or to cater? Actually, it's not necessary to make it an either/or situation. You might choose to do both: Cook a specialty dish or two using your Cuisinart® party-mates and then supplement your menu with items from a caterer or the take-out/delivery food service or even your favorite restaurant.

With your budget, serving style and theme in mind, select a menu you know your guests would enjoy. *Celebrations for Everyday and Special Occasions* offers a variety of enticing recipes to complement any entertaining menu.

Hosting Helper

When entertaining, never experiment with a recipe for a new dish, especially if it's the main course. Instead, try it out on your spouse and a close friend or two to avoid a "new recipe nightmare" at your perfectly planned gathering. However, even with the best cooks, plans can go awry. A soufflé may fall flat or a roast might be burned – essentially ruining the dish. If this happens, understand that your guests are there to see you, not to judge your cooking skills. There's no shame in calling in your Cuisinart® cavalry to the rescue to help you whip up eggs and bacon for the bunch. It will be a newlywed memory that will bring smiles to your faces whenever it's later recalled. Plus, you'll receive kudos for keeping cool during your culinary calamity.

Service with a Smile

Repeat to yourself, "I can't do it all. I can't do it all." With a full schedule of home chores, work, extended family obligations, hobbies and possibly parenting duties, it's not surprising you may sometimes feel overwhelmed. Now is the time to recruit your spouse to help you.

Hosting Helper

For a formal occasion, if you are really strapped for time, find paid or volunteer help to manage your party and/or perform serving duties to free you to concentrate on your guests and fully enjoy your own event.

Strike Up the Band

Set the mood with the right music to match your occasion and create the intended feel. For a more formal event, you may want to consider live music.

Put It In Writing

For a large formal celebration, you will want to create three party plans for yourself: a *pre-party* list, a *during-the-party* list, and a *post-party* list.

For a casual occasion, choose the items from the lists that pertain to the event and style of celebration.

The *pre-party* list contains items to order and details to take care of well before and immediately before a party such as:

- Choosing the party area
- Creating your guest list
- Selecting a theme, if any
- Ordering, writing and sending invitations as well as collecting responses
- Securing rentals or borrowing needed items
- Choosing a menu and, if necessary, arranging for catering, serving help and/or purchasing and preparing food
- Planning and arranging for the proper entertainment and activities
- Selecting, ordering and/or creating party favors, prizes and/or gifts
- Arranging for guest parking, if necessary
- Preparing the party site

- Selecting and ordering décor
- Installing décor and setting the table
- Preparing food

To create your timeline, select one of the first items you must do, whether it's locating a piano player or ordering custom invitations. Work backwards from the party date so that you allow enough time to accomplish the goal. Be specific. For instance, don't just write "invitations" on your timetable. Schedule each step of the process such as:

- Shop for, create, and/or order invitations
- Address and mail the invitations
- Receive or track down responses

The key to creating a successful party is to plan it like a pro. Follow this example for each party component and you will relieve yourself of any hosting anxiety due to sloppy scheduling.

The *during-the-party* list is the timeframe of the party itself. Schedule your time for the hours before the party starts until the last guest leaves. This schedule can include such items as:

- Last minute food and cleaning preparations
- Getting yourself ready
- Instructing hired or volunteer help
- Starting music, dimming lights, lighting candles or any last-minute preparation needed to set the scene
- Greeting guests, handling coats, gifts, pot luck dishes, etc.
- Timing of food service, entertainment, activities, distributing applicable prizes and possibly staged photos
- Ending the party, distributing appropriate borrowed dishes and/or leftovers to guests and possibly giving out party favors
- Saying goodnight to guests
- Post-event clean-up

Hosting Helper

Schedule a half hour before the party begins for you to relax and get yourself centered, and always allot twice as much time as you think you need to complete a task.

This second list should be given to all of the people involved with hosting or serving your guests.

The *post-party* plan should contain a task schedule for doing the following:

- Cleaning up the party site
- Returning rentals and/or borrowed or lost items in a timely manner
- Sending thank you notes to all applicable vendors or helpers
- Organizing your notes and resources to make your next party run even more smoothly

Inviting Ideas:

- Depending on the type of party, casual or formal, choose the style of invitation that works best for your event.
- Formal occasions, themed events or other types of parties which have a lot of detail such as instructions for guest dress, directions, surprise party information and so on, should be written, not given orally.
- Each invitation should include the 5 W's: Who, what, when, where and why.
- Buy custom invitations at a party supply store, stationery store, or print shop. Or, create invitations on your computer or by hand with plain or decorative invitation stock.
- For casual and last minute events, it is perfectly acceptable (if not common), to invite your guests in person or via telephone or e-mail.

Remember, the invitation is your guest's first clue to what awaits them at the party so be sure it creates excitement from the moment it arrives and is opened.

Neither Rain, Nor Sleet, Nor…

Here's the timeline to follow when using traditional methods to send your invitations:

- Invitations to costumed theme events or milestone occasions (weddings, anniversaries, christenings, a Bris, milestone birthdays and so on) or parties on weekends during the busy holiday season should be sent four to six weeks in advance.

Hosting Helper

If you are inviting out-of-town guests to a wedding, reunion or milestone celebration, send a save-the-date card soon after you set the date so they can make arrangements to attend. Then, follow up with a traditional invitation as previously described.

- If you choose to use a printed invitation for a casual event, they can be sent out two to three weeks in advance.

Can You Make It?

When sending an invitation for a celebration, include the R.S.V.P. date and contact information.

Never have four letters caused as much confusion as these: R.S.V.P. is the abbreviation for *repondez, s'il vous plait* in French or "please respond," in English.

Help your guests by keeping it simple. Either offer a phone number to call or enclose a reply card with the words "Please Respond By" and include a date a week or two before your party. If you don't hear from a guest(s), you can follow up with a telephone call and still provide yourself with enough time to make final party arrangements.

Party Pantry

In addition to the beautiful Cuisinart® hosting-helpers you have put on your gift registry, here are some other items to put on your wish list or to acquire on your own.

Stocking the Bar

The right beverage glasses are not only necessary to show your good taste but also help drinks taste their best. Here is a list of the basic glassware you should own:

Glasses
- Highball glasses (8 to 12 ounces)
- Old-fashioned or on-the-rocks glasses (6 to 8 ounces)
- Stemmed, white wine glasses (6 to 8 ounces)
- Large, stemmed, red wine glasses (8 to 10 ounces)

Hosting Helper

If you can't afford both red and white wine glasses, the large bowl on the red wine glass can work for both red and white wine and also serve as a water goblet.

Here are some other glasses you will eventually want to acquire:

- Beer mugs
- Brandy snifters
- Cordial glasses
- Fluted champagne glasses
- Irish coffee mugs
- Margarita glasses
- Martini glasses
- Pilsner beer glasses
- Punch glasses
- Whiskey sour glasses

In addition to your Cuisinart® blender, you'll need the following tools to help you earn your degree as a master mixologist:

- Bar knife
- Bottle/can opener
- Cocktail strainer
- Corkscrew
- Ice bucket
- Ice tongs
- Jigger for measuring
- Long-necked stirrer
- Martini shaker
- Measuring spoons
- Muddler (for Mint Juleps and other similar drinks which require ingredients to be tamped)
- Small pitcher or carafe for water or wine
- Wine/champagne bucket

- Wine decanter
- Wine charms or tags

Let's Dish

Whether you buy dishes in a set, by the piece or by place setting, your basic needs for each guest include:

- Dinner plate
- Salad/bread and butter/dessert plate(s)
- Soup bowl
- Cup and saucer

Over time you will also want to acquire the following additions:

- Charger or service plates (Large, decorative platters put at each place setting under the dinner plate. It is generally removed when the first course is served or the first course plate may be placed on it. Food is never directly served on a charger.)
- Luncheon plates
- Serving bowls (with and without covers) and platters

Put a Fork In It

Whether acquired in sets or by the piece, you will need the following flatware pieces for each place setting of basic dining service:

- Dinner fork
- Salad/dessert fork
- Serrated dinner knife
- Tablespoon/place spoon (as a soup spoon substitute)
- Teaspoon/dessert spoon

For more formal occasions you will eventually want to acquire the following flatware for each guest as well:

- Butter knife
- Fish fork
- Soup spoon
- Steak knife

At Your Service

Gracious dining requires the following matching or coordinating serving pieces and utensils:

- Cake cutter/server
- Gravy boat
- Meat fork
- Pie cutter/server
- Salad dressing cruets
- Serving fork
- Slotted spoon
- Small ladle (for serving gravy or salad dressing from a bowl instead of the preferred gravy boat or small carafe)
- Multiple salt and pepper shaker sets

Hosting Helper

For true elegance, purchase tiny salt and pepper shakers for each guest's place setting.

Topping the Table

- Except for the most informal occasions, paper or plastic tablecloths, napkins or place mats should not be used.

- Starched, cotton napkins will hold a decorative fold better than ones made of synthetic fibers. And while synthetic fibers will retain their color better, they also are more apt to hold stains as well.

- To-the-floor linens are more elegant than cloths with a shorter drop.

- Overlays, or a second, possibly transparent or shorter cloth, will add texture and style when placed over a long cloth.

Hosting Helper

Overlays also provide versatility to a neutral, to-the-floor tablecloth to give you more uses throughout the year.

- Runners can be used to protect wooden tables from scratches caused by a centerpiece, hot plates or watermarks.
- For semi-formal or casual occasions, placemats can be combined with runners.
- Liquid-absorbing coasters protect your furniture from water stains and scratches.
- Trivets keep very hot platters or bowls from marring your dining or buffet table.

Décor Galore and Rental Realities

Match your party décor to your theme or occasion for the full "wow" factor. Until you acquire everything you need or have a reliable source from which you can borrow, find the best rental agency in your area. They can provide you with tables, chairs, linens, glassware, dishes, serving pieces and other hosting essentials in a wide variety of styles and colors, suitable for the most formal or casual occasions. Plus, by taking advantage of rental items, for just a few dollars, you can mix and match items with your own pieces to create a new designer touch for each occasion.

Center of Attention

While flowers are always correct, get creative with crafts. Put together a grouping of objets d'art, candles, framed photos, collectibles, or anything that you want to use to add charm as a centerpiece on your table setting, your buffet or to reinforce a theme.

Hosting Helper

Be sure that any centerpiece is placed below or raised above the eye-level of your guests (approximately 16 inches) so as not to interfere with conversation.

Can I Borrow…?

Shakespeare wrote "Neither a borrower or lender be." Nonsense! If you have a need for an item or items to create the type of atmosphere you desire, and a friend or relative owns just the right thing and is willing to loan it, by all means, borrow away.

Preparing Your Place

Don't let a less-than-spotless home keep you from entertaining. A thorough cleaning of every nook, cranny and closet, while nice, is not always essential.

Remember, this is not a visit by the Clean Police. You can go for the "illusion" of clean. Close off rooms that are less than company ready. Then, remove clutter and give your furniture and floors a good dusting, mopping and/or vacuuming. Clean your bathrooms and other areas where guests will gather and then forget about it.

It's Outta Here

While it's nice to show off prized possessions and family heirlooms, if you're concerned that favorite pieces may become jostled or broken during a large gathering, remove them. You can always put them back on display when there are fewer guests in the room.

Keep It Clean

Watch any televised cooking show and the chef always has all the ingredients neatly assembled in small bowls or on plates. If you have an open floor plan where guests can watch while you cook or, if people always pile into your kitchen while you're cooking, this type of early preparation can help you prepare even the most complicated meal with a minimum of mess.

Hosting Helper

For even less stress and mess, prepare and pre-measure your needed ingredients and put them into disposable plastic bags and bowls. Pour the ingredients into your recipes as needed and dispose of the bags and bowls. No muss, no fuss.

Another tactic is to keep a sink full of hot, soapy water to wash plates and pots as you work. Or simply rinse your bowls and utensils and slip them into your dishwasher for a later washing.

If possible, store any dishes you can make hours or days before in a container in which you can quickly re-heat and/or serve the item. The elegant design of many of your Cuisinart® cooking pieces make them perfect to go straight from your stove to your table.

For spills that you and/or a guest may make, have a cloth handy for absorbing the mess. After the party, use a cleaner to spot the spill more completely.

Service With Style

As the saying goes, it's not what you do but how you do it. In this section we'll cover some fine points of graceful living you'll want to keep in mind and items you should acquire to serve with style.

Style Essentials

- A fully loaded, wicker picnic basket, complete with plates, glassware and flatware can turn even take-out sandwiches into a romantic repast.
- A footed tray is perfect for breakfast in bed, writing thank-you letters or to serve a celebration meal to your "private" guest of honor.
- A variety of vases to hold a simple bud or a bountiful bouquet.
- Napkin rings can add style or reinforce a theme without the time or skill needed to make fancy folds.

Have a Seat

- For formal occasions, or the times when there are many guests around the table, placecards are a graceful way to help guests find their seat.
- Create the cards with a small piece of folded, heavy card stock and hand or computer-printed calligraphy.
- Paint names on colorful real or ceramic eggs for an Easter, Passover or Sunday brunch.
- Carve names into a mini pumpkin for Halloween, a Fall feast or Thanksgiving.

Hosting Helper

When placing people at your table, seat a gregarious guest next to a shy one to draw that person out. Split up couples to encourage livelier conversations.

A unique placecard can serve double-duty as a party favor. Your choice of options is limited only by your imagination.

Left Is Right

Food is always served from the left and picked up from the right. The logic behind this tradition is that most people are right-handed and left-sided service makes it easier for them to serve themselves.

Hosting Helper

To remember whether forks, knives and spoons go on the right or left side of the plate, the word "left" has four letters and so does "fork." "Spoon" and "knife" each have five letters and so does the word "right." The only exception is a fish fork, which is placed on the right side of the plate. Flatware is always placed so that the first piece needed for a meal is on the far left or right of the plate, so flatware is used from the outside in.

Here's another trick. Form an "ok" sign with your left and right hand. You'll note that your left hand resembles a small "b" and your right hand looks like a "d." Therefore, a **b**read plate should go on the top left side of a place setting and **d**rinks should go on the top right.

Forget-Me-Not

Let guests remember the fun of your gathering by giving them a party favor suited to the occasion. Whether usable, wearable, or edible, it doesn't have to be expensive. It's just a thoughtful gesture to let guests know how much you enjoyed their company.

Hints and Helpers – A "Hosting Helper Refresher Course"

- Saying "thank you" is expected when you receive a gift or thoughtful gesture. Sending a hand-written (not e-mailed), thank-you note makes the giver feel truly appreciated.
- Shortly after guests arrive, offer them a drink and something to eat.
- Never serve a round bowl, like a soup or salad bowl, without a flat plate under it.
- When dispensing beverages or finger foods, always supply a clean cocktail napkin with each serving. Have small trash containers

available in your party space for guests to throw away soiled napkins. Empty these containers often.

- If you are passing hors d'oeuvres with toothpicks, be sure to have a small bowl or tray for guests to dispose of used picks.

- Even if you are childless, be prepared for small-fry guests. Purchase a couple of coloring books and rent a few age-appropriate videos or video games to keep children occupied. Don't forget to have child-friendly foods on hand.

Hosting Helper

A quick call to the child's parents will either result in their bringing their own toys and treats or at least giving you a clue to what the child would like.

- Always have tasty and attractive non-alcoholic drinks available for designated drivers.

- For potluck parties, assign specific food or beverage items as you receive guest responses and after seeking the guest's preference. This will enable you to avoid duplication of dishes and to plan a well-balanced and coordinated menu.

- Encourage guests to bring menu items that can be quickly warmed in the microwave, offered chilled or served at room temperature, rather than selecting a dish that requires last-minute preparation in your already-busy kitchen.

- To inhibit the growth of bacteria and to avoid food poisoning, food should be kept at above 140°F or below 40°F. Don't let food sit out for longer than an hour (less time in warm areas) unless it's kept directly on ice or heat. Even then, it is better to serve smaller portions that are replaced, not replenished, frequently with fresh food. Otherwise guests might have a not-so-pleasant memory of your party.

Here are some tips for how to handle some typical and sticky situations:

- If someone asks, "May I bring a guest?" and it will adversely affect your plans, tactfully explain your space limitations or the fact that it is a personal occasion designed for only those who are "close" to the guest of honor.

- If an unexpected guest appears on your party's doorstep, gracefully make additional room without slighting any of your invited guests. It is an awkward situation, but you can get through it if you stay calm and seek a creative adjustment to your plans.

- If a dinner guest is late to arrive, it is not necessary to delay your perfectly timed dinner and inconvenience your other, more timely guests. Graciously welcome the late-comer and help him or her to catch up.

- Call a taxi or arrange alternate transportation for any guest who over-imbibes, no matter how much they resist your efforts.

Goodies-to-Go Hints

Here are some tips for keeping food fresh and delicious for parties on the move:

- When bringing party provisions to a friend's house, wrap food in decorative, but disposable platters or in covered bowls. Write your name on masking tape and place the tape on the bottom of any containers you wish returned.

- To keep food hot while transporting, cover containers with foil, then wrap in heavy towels and place in an empty thermal cooler or container.

- Put cut vegetables for a crudités platter in sealed, plastic bags or covered plastic bowls with a dampened paper towel. Place on ice in a cooler or refrigerate to keep crisp until serving.

Formal place setting

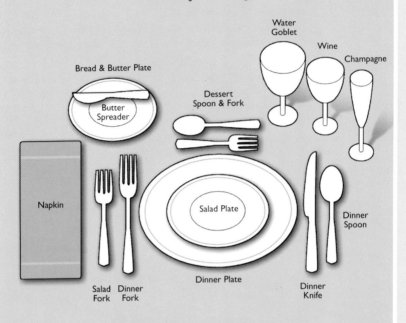

Bread & Butter Plate

Butter Spreader

Water Goblet

Wine

Champagne

Dessert Spoon & Fork

Napkin

Salad Plate

Dinner Spoon

Salad Fork

Dinner Fork

Dinner Plate

Dinner Knife

Chapter 3

Celebrating the Moments Just for Two

Just because it's only the two of you doesn't mean that you shouldn't celebrate frequently and spontaneously. Adding special little touches to everyday meals will help keep the spark in your marriage. After all, isn't it worth the effort to treat each other as hospitably and lovingly as you would your guests?

Bright Breakfast Ideas

Mornings. Who has time for breakfast? You do! With your Cuisinart® programmable coffee pot and other small appliances, you can whip up a tasty meal in minutes. Whether you're inviting family and friends for a weekend breakfast or brunch, or you're whipping up a hearty and healthy breakfast for two before you both dash to work, your Cuisinart® appliances and *Celebrations for Everyday and Special Occasions* are here to help.

When busy mornings arrive filled with appointments and commitments, make "fast" and "fortifying" your breakfast bywords. On days when you have no time for a leisurely breakfast, you can quickly whip up healthy fruit smoothies in your Cuisinart® blender. This time-saving tip allows you to sit, sip and share the plans for the day. Even when your time is limited, add a few decorative details to your morning dash out the door, and start your morning off on a bright note.

Speedy Service with Style

- Play lively music to add a bounce to your breakfast.
- Serve smoothies in tall crystal goblets.

- Put out beautiful placemats and napkins
- Place a decorative timer nearby to keep you on your time-sensitive track.

WEEKDAY WHIRLWIND WAKE-UP MENU
(Highlighted recipes are included.)

Banana Berry Smoothies

or

Juice Bar Orange Smoothies

Coffee

Banana Berry Smoothies

2	ripe bananas, cut into 1-inch pieces
1 cup	strawberry halves or whole blueberries
1 cup	fresh orange juice
2/3 cup	fat-free vanilla yogurt
2 tablespoons	honey crunch wheat germ
1 cup	ice cubes

Place the ingredients in the blender jar of the Cuisinart® SmartPower Premier™ Blender in the order listed. Blend on High speed until smooth and frothy. Serve immediately.

Makes 2 servings.

Banana Berry Smoothie

Juice Bar Orange Juice Smoothies

4 strips	orange zest, bitter white pith removed
2 tablespoons	sugar
I cup	fresh orange segments, cut into I-inch pieces
I cup	fat-free milk
I cup	orange tangerine juice blend
1/2 cup	powdered fat-free milk
I teaspoon	powdered egg white
2 teaspoons	vanilla extract
15	ice cubes

Place the orange zest and half the sugar in blender jar of the Cuisinart® SmartPower Premier™ Blender. Set on Low and blend for 10 to 15 seconds. Add the remaining ingredients to the blender jar in the order listed. Cover the blender jar. Set on High and cover and blend until smooth and slushy, about 20 to 30 seconds. Serve immediately.

Makes 4 servings.

Weekends

Weekends are a great time to share the cooking duties and then to sit and savor breakfast at your kitchen counter, in your dining room, on your terrace or in bed.

Breakfast in Bed

- Use a brightly colored linen tablecloth or a tray with a placemat and contrasting napkins.
- Serve coffee in decorative mugs and place your muffins or fruit on coordinating plates.
- Add sparkle to the setting with your good flatware.
- For added panache, pour juice into crystal goblets, place butter on a butter dish, and spoon your favorite gourmet jam into a small, decorative bowl before serving.
- Add fresh flowers in a pretty vase or a small, potted, flowering plant to complete the look.

MARVELOUS MORNING MENU

(Highlighted recipes are included.)

Coffee and juice

Sliced fruit

Pear & Cherry Coffee Cake

Souffléd Omelet with Cheddar, Bacon, Roasted Peppers and Avocado

Pear & Cherry Coffee Cake

	cooking spray
3 cups*	fresh pears, peeled, cored and cut into 1/8-inch slices
1	lemon, juiced
3/4 cup	brown sugar, firmly packed
1 tablespoon	ground cinnamon
1/2 teaspoon	nutmeg, freshly grated
1/2 cup	dried tart cherries
3 cups	all-purpose flour
1 tablespoon	baking powder
3/4 teaspoon	salt
2 cups	granulated sugar
1 cup	unsalted butter, cut into 1/2-inch pieces
4 large	eggs
2 teaspoons	pure vanilla extract

Preheat the oven to 350°F. Lightly coat the Cuisinart® Roast and Bake Pan with cooking spray. Place the pears, lemon juice, brown sugar, cinnamon, nutmeg and dried cherries in a medium bowl. Toss gently to combine and set aside.

Place the flour, baking powder and salt in a medium bowl. Use the Cuisinart® Electronic Hand Mixer on Speed 1 to aerate the flour mixture for 15 seconds. Set aside.

Place the sugar and butter in a large mixing bowl and mix on Speed 3, creaming until well-blended. Add the eggs and vanilla on Speed 3 and mix for 50 seconds. Add the flour mixture. Blend on Speed 1 for 1 minute or until the batter is smooth. The batter will be very thick. Spread two-thirds of the batter evenly in the bottom of the pan. Scatter the fruit and spice mixture evenly over the batter. Spoon the remaining batter randomly over the fruit. Bake for 55 to 60 minutes, or until a tester inserted in the center of the cake comes out clean. Cool the cake in the pan on a wire rack for at least 30 minutes before cutting. Wrap tightly and refrigerate any leftovers.

Makes 18 to 24 servings.

*About 1 1/2 pounds fresh pears before trimming.

Souffléd Omelet with Cheddar, Bacon, Roasted Peppers & Avocado

2 slices	lean bacon, cut into 1/2-inch pieces
	cooking spray
3 large	eggs, separated
1 1/2 tablespoons	all-purpose flour
1/8 teaspoon	salt
pinch	freshly ground pepper
dash	bottled hot sauce (optional)
pinch	cream of tartar
1 ounce	reduced-fat cheddar cheese, shredded and divided in half
1/2	roasted red pepper, cut in 1/2-inch pieces
1/4	ripe avocado, peeled and diced

Preheat the oven to 375°F. Sauté the bacon in the Cuisinart® 8-inch Skillet over low heat until crispy. Remove the bacon to a paper towel and drain. Discard the grease. Wash and dry the skillet. Coat the cooking surface of the clean skillet with cooking spray.

Please the egg yolks, flour, salt, pepper and hot sauce, if using, in a medium bowl. Use the Cuisinart® Electric Hand Mixer to beat the egg yolk mixture until it is thick and lemon-colored and set aside. Clean the beaters completely. Place the egg whites in a spotlessly clean glass, stainless or copper bowl. Whip the egg whites with the cream of tartar until they are shiny and hold stiff peaks. Stir about one-third of the beaten egg whites into the egg yolks. Gently fold the remaining egg whites into the yolks and pour the omelet into the prepared skillet. Bake the omelet in the oven until puffed and golden brown, about 11 to 12 minutes. Top with half of the cheese and continue baking for 2 minutes.

Remove the omelet from the oven and top with the remaining cheese, bacon, red peppers and avocado. Serve immediately. You may also serve the omelet with salsa, if desired.

Makes 2 servings.

A Loving Lunch

Back-to-back appointments, late nights, missed meals. Will you ever find time to be together? A lunchtime picnic at a nearby park or even in the office might be just what you need to rev up your romance.

Remember, your Cuisinart® appliances can make quick work of a romantic mid-day repast. So, perk up your plans with these delightful details:

- Pack a thermal bag with your lunch and place it inside a picnic basket fully loaded with plates, glassware and flatware.
- Bring along a tablecloth or picnic blanket and decorative napkins, as well as salt and pepper shakers.
- To add music to your meal, take along a portable CD player and your favorite songs.

LAKESIDE LUNCH MENU
(Highlighted recipes are included.)

Spicy Vegetable Wraps with Cucumber-Mint Sauce

Brie

Asian pears

Sweetened iced tea

Spicy Vegetable Wraps with Cucumber-Mint Sauce

2 medium	cucumbers, peeled, halved, seeded, cut to fit large feed tube vertically
1 teaspoon	salt
1/2 cup	fresh mint leaves
1/2 cup	plain nonfat yogurt
	black pepper to taste
1 small	jalapeño pepper, seeded, cut into 4 pieces
1 medium	red onion, peeled, one end cut flat
1 medium	red bell pepper, cored, cut into 3 pieces
1 medium	yellow bell pepper, cored, cut into 3 pieces
1 large	carrot, peeled, cut to fit into large feed tube horizontally
4	9 to 10-inch flour tortillas
	cooking spray

Place the cucumber pieces in the Cuisinart® Food Processor fitted with the medium shredding disc and shred using light pressure. Transfer to a colander and sprinkle with the salt. Toss to coat and drain for 20 minutes. Rinse, squeeze out the excess moisture and pat the cucumber until dry. Place in a medium bowl. Insert the metal blade and process the mint until finely chopped, about 10 seconds. Add the mint to the cucumber, along with the yogurt and black pepper. Stir to combine. Divide the sauce in half and chill until ready to serve.

Using the metal blade, process the jalapeño pepper until finely chopped, about 10 seconds. Insert the 2mm slicing disc and place the onion in the large feed tube, cut side down. Slice, using medium pressure and set aside. Insert the 4mm slicing disc and place the pepper pieces in the large feed tube horizontally. Slice, using light pressure and reserve. Insert the medium shredding disc. Place the carrot in the large feed tube horizontally and slice, using medium pressure. Coat a Cuisinart® Nonstick 12-inch Skillet with the cooking spray and place over medium-high heat. Add the onion and jalapeño and stir-fry for 4 to 5 minutes, or until soft but not brown. Add the pepper and carrot and sauté until crisp and tender, about 2 to 3 minutes.

Place one-fourth of the vegetables horizontally across the center of each tortilla, leaving a 2-inch border on the side closest to you. Using half of the reserved cucumber-mint sauce, distribute 1 tablespoon of sauce evenly over the vegetables. Fold the 2-inch border up and over the vegetable mixture, then fold in the sides and roll up to complete the wrap. Place the wraps in a Cuisinart® Nonstick 10-inch Skillet over medium heat. Cook for 2 to 3 minutes, turning once, until lightly browned on both sides. Serve with the remaining cucumber-mint sauce.

Makes 4 servings.

Tip: Wear disposable rubber gloves when handling jalapeño peppers.

Weekends

Weekends are our days to do errands, share household chores and to try out new recipes to make sure they're company ready. Here are a few ways to add luxury to your lunch and to test table décor ideas for upcoming company dinners.

Luxurious Lunch Table

- Set the table with your beautiful silverware, china and glassware. (Why save it for company-only occasions?)

- Add mealtime music and don't forget to take a spin around your dining room's dance floor.

LUXURIOUS LUNCH

(Highlighted recipes are included.)

Penne with Sun-Dried Tomato Vodka Sauce

Focaccia Romano

Iced tea

Penne with Sun-Dried Tomato Vodka Sauce

I teaspoon	unsalted butter
I teaspoon	extra virgin olive oil
2 cloves	garlic, peeled and chopped
I	shallot, peeled and chopped
3/4 teaspoon	dried thyme
I 1/2 cups	fresh plum tomatoes, peeled and diced (you may use canned
	unpeeled tomatoes, if desired)
3/4 ounce	sun-dried tomatoes packed without oil, chopped (about 6 halves)
3 tablespoons	vodka (I 1/2 ounces)
1/4 cup	light cream
1/8 teaspoon	dried, crushed red pepper (use bottled hot sauce, if desired)
I 1/2 cups	dry penne pasta
I small	zucchini, cleaned and thinly sliced
	fresh thyme and Italian parsley, chopped
	Reggiano Parmesan cheese, freshly grated

Pour 10 cups of water into the Cuisinart® 3 quart Sauce Pan and set aside. Add 1/2 teaspoon salt. Melt the butter with the olive oil in the Cuisinart® 2 quart Sauce Pan over medium heat. Add the onion and garlic and sauté until tender and translucent, about 2 minutes. Add the thyme and continue cooking for 1 minute. Add the plum tomatoes and sun-dried tomatoes and cook until most of the liquid has been absorbed, about 8 to 10 minutes. Add the cream, vodka and red pepper and continue cooking over medium-low heat for 10 minutes until the sauce has thickened.

Prepare the pasta by heating the water and salt to boiling. Add the penne and cook according to the package directions, until the pasta is cooked al denté. Add the zucchini during the last 2 minutes of cooking. Drain the pasta and zucchini, reserving one-fourth cup of the liquid. Add the penne and zucchini to the cream sauce and toss gently to coat completely, adding the pasta liquid as needed. Garnish the pasta with the fresh thyme and Italian parsley to taste and sprinkle the cheese over the herbs to taste. Serve immediately.

Makes 2 entrée servings or 4 to 6 side servings.

Focaccia Romana

1/4 ounce package	active dry yeast
1/8 teaspoon	sugar
1/3 cup	warm water (105°F to 115°F)
4 cups	all-purpose flour
1 teaspoon	salt
1 cup	cold water
4 tablespoons	extra virgin olive oil, divided
	cooking spray
2 teaspoons	coarse sea salt

Stir the yeast and sugar into the warm water in a 2-cup measuring cup. Let stand until foamy, about 3 to 5 minutes. Fit the dough blade in the Cuisinart® Food Processor and add the flour and salt. Process to combine, about 20 seconds. Add the cold water and 2 tablespoons of oil to the yeast mixture. While the Food Processor is running, pour the liquid through the feed tube in a steady stream as fast as flour absorbs it. When the dough pulls away from the sides of the work bowl, process until the dough is well kneaded, about 40 to 45 seconds.

Place the dough in a lightly floured plastic food storage bag. Let rise in a warm place until doubled in size, about 45 minutes. Divide the dough in half and place on a lightly floured surface. Roll each half into two 10-inch rounds. Coat two baking sheets with cooking spray and place the rounds on the baking sheets. Use kitchen shears to make decorative cuts in the dough. Pull the dough from the edges, opening the cuts to give a lattice-like appearance. Brush each round with the remaining olive oil and sprinkle with salt. Cover with plastic wrap sprayed with cooking spray and let rise until puffy, about 20 minutes. Preheat the oven to 450°F. Bake the focaccia until golden and crisp, about 20 to 25 minutes. Cool slightly on a wire rack. Serve warm.

Makes 18 servings.

Tip: Coarse sea salt is available in most supermarkets.
Look for it in the specialty food aisle.

Duo Dining

When possible, make dinner the time to unwind with each other, relate the day's events and talk about the future, whether its plans for the weekend, a vacation getaway or remodeling your new home. Combine your talents to prepare a delicious meal, set an attractive table and even add small, personal touches to make it a mini-celebration.

Soothing Seaside Spread

- Burn candles in hurricane lamps for an evening shimmer.
- Serve small appetizers on seashells or on seashell-shaped plates.
- Complete the ambiance with a CD of sea sounds.

FISH FEST FARE
(Highlighted recipes are included.)

Shrimp Cocktail

Pan-Seared Salmon with Tangerine Shallot Sauce

Garlic Mashed Potatoes

Steamed Mixed Vegetables

Lemon Frozen Yogurt

Pan-Seared Salmon with Tangerine Shallot Sauce

2	**fresh salmon fillets, 6 ounces each, with skin**
I teaspoon	**extra virgin olive oil**
1/4 teaspoon	**salt**
1/8 teaspoon	**freshly ground black pepper**
1/2 cup	**dry white vermouth**
1/2 cup	**fresh tangerine juice**
I tablespoon	**shallots, peeled and finely chopped**
I tablespoon	**heavy cream**

Rinse the salmon in cold water and pat dry with paper towels. Rub the salmon fillets with olive oil and sprinkle with salt and pepper. Heat the Cuisinart® 10-inch Stick-Free Skillet over medium-high heat. When the skillet is hot, but not smoking, add the salmon fillets, skin side up, in the skillet. Sear over medium-high heat for 4 minutes. Do not turn the fillets or move them as they cook. Turn the salmon and sear for 4 minutes. Transfer the salmon to a heated platter and cover loosely with aluminum foil. Do not overcook the salmon. It will continue cooking on the platter as it rests while you prepare the sauce.

Clean the pan with paper towels and add the wine, juice and shallots. Stir and cook over medium-high heat to reduce the liquid by two-thirds. Reduce the heat to low and slowly add the heavy cream, stirring to blend well. Continue stirring and cooking over low heat until the sauce is thickened and smooth. To serve, pour the sauce over each fillet and garnish with steamed snow peas, if desired.

Makes 2 servings.

Pan-Seared Salmon
with Tangerine Shallot Sauce

Lemon Frozen Yogurt

1 1/2 cups	granulated sugar
1 cup	fresh lemon juice
3 cups	plain lowfat yogurt
1 tablespoon	lemon zest, finely chopped

Combine the sugar and juice in the Cuisinart® 1 1/2 quart Saucepan and bring to a boil, stirring occasionally. Reduce the heat and simmer until the sugar is completely melted. Cool to room temperature. Refrigerate for 8 hours before using. Freeze the Cuisinart® Automatic Frozen Yogurt – Ice Cream & Sorbet Maker chiller bowl while chilling the syrup.

Add the yogurt and lemon zest to the chilled syrup and stir until completely blended. Pour the yogurt into the frozen chiller bowl and turn the Frozen Yogurt – Ice Cream & Sorbet Maker to On. Freeze for 25 to 30 minutes, or until the yogurt is thickened and has a soft, creamy texture. Turn the machine Off. Serve immediately or, if desired, transfer the frozen yogurt to an airtight container and place in the freezer for about 2 hours until firm. To serve, remove the frozen yogurt from the freezer 10 to 15 minutes before serving.

Makes 8 servings.

Lemon Frozen Yogurt

Once-a-Week Dinner Date

Experts say that the secret to a happy marriage is to schedule a weekly date. By planning ahead, you'll have the fun of anticipating your special time together. Even a night spent at home enjoying an exceptional dinner and then watching a video can take on a "date-like" atmosphere if you treat the night like a special occasion. Make it as exciting as your first date!

Reservations for Two

- If you normally eat in the kitchen, move the meal to your dining room. If your dining room is where meals are usually served, move it to your garden, terrace, living room or bedroom. String white twinkle lights to create your own starlit night. This small change in latitude will immediately improve your attitude.

- This date deserves an invitation. Write a note to your spouse and place it on his pillow or by the bathroom sink.

- Print out the menu on a decorative sheet of paper and place it on the table.

- In addition to an elegant table setting, candlelight, fresh flowers, soft music and loving banter are romantic requirements.

DINNER DATE DELICACIES
(Highlighted recipes are included.)

Tossed Baby Field Greens with an Oil and Vinaigrette Dressing

Lemon Herb Roast Chicken

Wild Rice With Shiitake Mushrooms and Pecans

Pink Grapefruit Sorbet

Red wine (merlot, cabernet or your choice)

Lemon Herb Roast Chicken

3 1/2 to 4 pounds	whole roasting chicken
3/4 teaspoon	salt
1/2 teaspoon	freshly ground black pepper
4-inch sprig	fresh herb of your choice (rosemary, thyme, oregano, etc.)
1 clove	garlic, peeled and cut in half
1 small	onion, peeled and quartered
4 strips	lemon zest (1/2" x 3" each)
1 tablespoon	extra virgin olive oil
1 tablespoon	freshly squeezed lemon juice

Place the rack in the Cuisinart® Convection Toaster Oven Broiler in Position A. Preheat the convection oven to 400°F.

Remove the giblets and neck from the cavity of the chicken and reserve for another use or discard. Rinse the chicken with cold water and pat dry with paper towels. Place the drip tray in the broiling pan in the lower position and lightly coat the drip tray with cooking spray. Pour one-fourth cup of water into the bottom of the broiling pan. Tuck the chicken wings in and place the chicken on the prepared drip tray.

Combine the salt and pepper and rub half of the mixture in the cavity of the chicken. Place the herb sprig, garlic, onion and lemon zest in the cavity of the chicken. Use white cotton or cooking string to loosely tie the legs together. Rub the skin of the chicken with olive oil and sprinkle the remaining salt and pepper over the chicken. Drizzle the lemon juice over the chicken. Clean the work surface and your hands with soap and hot water before continuing.

Roast the chicken for 20 minutes. Reduce the temperature to 375°F and continue roasting for an additional 12 minutes per pound. The internal temperature of the chicken should be 170°F when tested in the breast meat and 180°F when tested in the dark meat. When done, the juices should run clear.

When done, remove the roast chicken to a platter. Let stand 10 to 15 minutes before carving. If you prefer a crisp skin, let the chicken rest uncovered. If you prefer a soft skin, cover the chicken loosely with aluminum foil.

Makes 4 servings.

Wild Rice with Shiitake Mushrooms and Pecans

4 cups	water
3/4 cup	wild rice
2 tablespoons	margarine or butter, divided
1/2 cup	pecans
1 rib	celery, peeled, trimmed, cut into 1-inch pieces
1 small	onion, peeled and quartered
3 ounces	shiitake mushrooms, cleaned, stems trimmed
1/4 teaspoon	ground black pepper
1/4 teaspoon	salt

Pour the water into the Cuisinart® 3 quart sauce pan. Bring to a boil over medium-high heat. Reduce the heat to low and add the rice. Simmer, partially covered, for about 30 minutes or until tender. While rice is cooking, melt 1 1/2 tablespoons of the margarine in the Cuisinart® 3 1/2 Quart Sauté Pan over medium heat. Add the pecans and toast, stirring often, until lightly browned, about 5 minutes. Cool slightly. Place the pecans in the Cuisinart® Food Processor fitted with the metal blade and pulse to coarsely chop, about 6 times. Set aside. Coarsely chop the celery and onion, pulsing about 4 to 5 times. Leave the vegetables in work bowl and insert the standard slicing disc. Place the mushrooms in the large feed tube and slice using light pressure. About 5 minutes before the rice is done, heat the remaining 1 tablespoon margarine in the sauté pan over medium heat. Add the vegetables and sauté for 3 to 4 minutes, stirring occasionally. Drain the rice. Add the rice and pecans to skillet and cook until heated through, about 3 to 4 minutes. Season with pepper and salt to taste and serve warm.

Makes 6 servings.

Tip: Do not use water to clean mushrooms.
Simply brush off any loose dirt with a mushroom brush or clean towel.

Pink Grapefruit Sorbet

2 cups	**sugar**
2 cups	**water**
1 1/2 cups	**fresh pink grapefruit juice**
1 tablespoon	**grapefruit zest, finely grated**

Combine the sugar and water in the Cuisinart® Stainless 2 Quart Saucepan and bring to a boil over medium-high heat. Reduce the heat to low and simmer until the sugar dissolves, about 3 to 4 minutes. Stir occasionally. Cool completely by placing the liquid in a covered container and refrigerating overnight, or, if you wish to make the sorbet right away, chill the liquid over an ice bath for 30 minutes.

Add the grapefruit juice and zest and stir to combine. Pour the sorbet into the frozen freezer bowl of the Cuisinart® Frozen Yogurt – Ice Cream & Sorbet Maker. Turn the machine On and freeze until slushy, about 25 to 30 minutes. Transfer to an airtight container and place in the freezer until firm, about 2 hours.

Makes 8 1/2-cup servings.

Tip: The zest is the colored part of the citrus rind. Remove the zest with a vegetable peeler, avoiding the bitter white pith of the fruit.

Pink Grapefruit Sorbet

Chapter 4

Celebrating the Occasions

Outdoor Entertaining Essentials

As soon as the warm weather arrives after a long, cold and gray winter, it is the perfect time to dine alfresco, or outdoors. It's also the ideal reason to gather family and friends together to enjoy the balmy breezes and a patio picnic. Here's a delightful design for your springtime soiree.

Spring Summons

- Write your invitation on stationery that is bordered with a red and white gingham design.

Alfresco Adornments

- For evening events, light tiki torches, white or red pillar candles with glass hurricane covers, lanterns and/or luminarias to make your garden glow.

- String white twinkle lights in bushes and on trees, or entwine them in your table's umbrella, and set to a blinking mode so the lights appear to be fireflies.

- For country charm, use red and white gingham, or a blue denim tablecloth on your patio or picnic table as the backdrop for your meal.

- Roll white napkins and tie with red or blue gingham ribbon. If you're using a denim tablecloth, select a gingham napkin and tie with white or red ribbon.

- Place daisies and daffodils in a metal camping pitcher, a white tin coffee pot or a crockery pitcher for your country-style centerpiece.

- Red or blue-handled flatware will contrast nicely with your gingham or denim tablecloth.
- Red or cobalt blue dishes and coordinating glassware will add to your rustic atmosphere.

Spring Souvenirs

- Clay pots filled with fresh herbs
- A variety of vegetable seed packets
- Travel-size umbrellas
- Vinyl rain ponchos

MARVELOUS MENU
(Highlighted recipes are included.)

Green Salad with Tomato Vinaigrette

Grilled Flank Steak & Portobellos

Glazed Garden Vegetables with Fresh Herbs
(served in a covered vegetable dish to help keep food warm)

Simple Chocolate Cookie Ice Cream
(served in parfait glasses with chocolate sauce,
non-dairy topping, chocolate sprinkles, crushed cookies, nuts and
maraschino cherries for do-it-yourself ice cream toppers)

Iced tea

Grilled Flank Steak & Portobellos

2 pounds	beef flank steak
1 pound	Portobello mushrooms, cleaned, sliced 1/2-inch thick
1/2 cup	light soy sauce
1/3 cup	rice wine flavored vinegar
1/4 cup	dry or medium sherry
1/2 ounce	fresh ginger, finely chopped
1 teaspoon	Asian sesame oil (toasted sesame oil)
1 teaspoon	flavorless vegetable oil

Trim any excess fat from the steak and lightly score the steak with a sharp knife on both sides in a diagonal crosshatch pattern. The cuts should be about 1 to 1 1/2 inches apart. This prevents the beef from curling as it cooks. Place the meat in a self-sealing, heavy duty food storage bag and the mushrooms in a second bag. Combine the soy sauce, vinegar, sherry, ginger and sesame oil. Pour all of the marinade over the mushrooms and toss to coat. Pour the excess marinade over the steak and toss to coat. Seal both bags and marinate at room temperature for 30 minutes.

Preheat the Cuisinart® 12-inch Skillet over medium-high heat. When hot, brush with the vegetable oil. Arrange half of the mushroom slices in a single layer on the pan and sauté for 2 to 3 minutes on each side until tender. Do not move the mushrooms around on the pan while sautéing. Remove and transfer the mushrooms to a bowl. Add any remaining marinade from the mushrooms to the cooked mushrooms and cook the remaining mushrooms as directed above.

Drain the excess marinade from the flank steak and discard the marinade. Cook the beef in the hot skillet for 5 to 8 minutes per side, depending on your cooking preferences. When tested with an instant-read thermometer, the beef will register 120 to 125°F for rare, 125 to 140°F for medium rare, 145 to 155°F for medium and 160°F + for well done. Do not move the steak as it cooks, except to turn once. Remove the beef to a cutting board and let rest for 10 to 15 minutes before slicing. Cut the beef diagonally into thin slices against the grain of the beef. Arrange the meat on a platter and surround with the sautéed mushrooms. Pour the accumulated juices from the sautéed meat and mushrooms over all and serve at once.

Makes 8 servings.

Glazed Garden Vegetables with Fresh Herbs

1 tablespoon	**extra virgin olive oil**
1 red onion	**peeled and cut in 1/2-inch wedges**
2	**red bell peppers, cored, seeded and cut in 1/2-inch slices**
1	**yellow bell pepper, cored, seeded, cut in 1/2-inch slices**
12 ounces	**zucchini (1 1/4 inch or less in diameter) cut in 1/2-inch slices**
12 ounces	**yellow squash (1 1/4 inch or less in diameter) cut in 1/2-inch slices**
1/2 teaspoon	**salt**
2 tablespoons	**white balsamic or fruit flavored vinegar**
1/4 cup	**loosely packed mixed fresh herbs, chopped (parsley, tarragon, thyme, rosemary, etc.)**
1/4 teaspoon	**freshly ground black pepper**

Place the oil in a Cuisinart® 5 1/2 Quart Sauté Pan over medium-high heat. When hot, add the onions and peppers. Sauté about 3 to 4 minutes. Add the squash and salt. Continue cooking until tender and lightly golden brown, stirring occasionally, about 8 to 10 minutes. Add the vinegar and reduce until it is a glaze; stir in the reserved chopped fresh herbs and the pepper. Serve hot.

Note: Using a Cuisinart® Food Processor to do your chopping and slicing will make preparation go quickly.

Makes 8 servings.

Simple Chocolate Cookie Ice Cream

2 cups	**heavy cream, chilled**
1 cup	**whole milk, chilled**
3/4 cup	**sugar**
1 teaspoon	**vanilla extract**
1/2 cup	**chocolate sandwich cookies, crushed**

Place the heavy cream, milk, sugar and vanilla extract in a medium mixing bowl and combine until well blended. Pour into a frozen freezer bowl of the Cuisinart® Automatic Frozen Yogurt – Ice Cream & Sorbet Maker. Turn the machine On and freeze until the ice cream thickens, about 20 to 25 minutes. Add the crushed cookies to the ice cream during last 5 to 10 minutes of freezing. Transfer the ice cream to an airtight container and place in the freezer until firm, about 2 hours.

Makes 10 1/2-cup servings.

Tip: You may substitute whipping cream for heavy cream, however the texture of the frozen ice cream will not be as smooth. You may also substitute your favorite cookies to create a unique flavor of ice cream.

Warming a Home with Friends and Family

Whether celebrating your new or remodeled home, or helping friends with their open house by providing some festive foods, here are ideas to make your new home (or theirs) feel truly warm.

Invitations by Design

- Pen invitations onto the back of paint color sample cards.
- Create a collage border of magazine cutouts of interior design items (paintbrushes, rollers, rulers, furniture, blueprints, fabrics and so on) on your invitation stock. Print your invitation in the center of the sheet, then duplicate on a color copier.

Fanciful Furnishings

- Apply a felt backing to extra tiles used in the home for use as trivets, coasters or hors d'oeuvre trays.
- Display enlarged "before" and "after" photos of your new construction or renovation so that guests can see the changes.
- Set a small stepladder on the buffet table and use its steps as a riser to serve desserts, drinks or canapés.
- After a remodeling job, show off the tools of your labor by serving food in new paint buckets and/or paint trays. Use mini paint brushes to dispense condiments.
- A clean paint can will serve as a whimsical vase for flowers.
- Make paper rings out of new wallpaper for use as napkin holders.

HOME-COOKED CUISINE

(Highlighted recipes are included.)

Vegetable Crudités

Cajun Pork Roast (see tips for transporting hot food in Chapter 2)

Parmesan Breadsticks

Glazed Pear Upside-Down Cake

Tip: If you're traveling to a friends' house with this delicious cake, keep it in its cake pan until you reach your destination. Bring along a platter for serving and additional sliced pears for garnish. This will ensure nothing happens to it while it's being transported to the party.

Cajun Pork Roast — page 49

Cajun Pork Roast

4 tablespoons	sweet paprika
1 1/2 tablespoons	salt
1 tablespoon	sugar
1	bay leaf, roughly broken
1 tablespoon	garlic powder
1 tablespoon	minced dry onions
1 tablespoon	freshly ground black pepper
1/2 to 1 tablespoon	ground cayenne pepper
1 tablespoon	ground oregano
2 teaspoons	ground thyme
1 1/2 teaspoons	ground basil
1 teaspoon	ground rosemary
1/2 teaspoon	ground allspice
3 to 3 1/2 pounds	boneless pork loin roast, tied, about 12-inches in length
	cooking spray

To make the *Cajun Spice Rub,* place the spices and herbs in a Cuisinart® Mini-Prep® Plus Processor. Process until the spices and herbs are finely ground and no traces of the bay leaf remain. Transfer to a jar with a tight fitting lid for storage.

Rub the roast with 1 1/2 to 2 teaspoons of the *Cajun Spice Rub.* (If desired, the roast may be seasoned up to 1 day ahead of roasting. Wrap loosely in waxed paper to store in the coolest part of the refrigerator on a plate until ready to use. Allow the roast to sit at room temperature for 30 minutes before roasting).

Place the rack in the Cuisinart® Convection Toaster Oven Broiler in Position A. Preheat the convection oven to 400°F. Arrange the rack in the drip pan in the highest position and coat the rack lightly with cooking spray. Center the roast on the rack and roast for 15 minutes. Reduce the temperature to 325°F and continue roasting for an additional 35 to 45 minutes, or until the temperature is 155 to 160°F when tested with a meat thermometer. Transfer the roast to a warm platter and let rest for 10 minutes before slicing.

Slice the roast into 1/4-inch thick slices, or as preferred. Cover and refrigerate all leftovers.

If your Cuisinart® Toaster Oven Broiler does not have the Convection setting, use the Bake setting. Follow the directions above and increase the cooking time to 55 to 65 minutes.

Makes 8 servings.

Glazed Pear Upside-Down Cake

6 tablespoons	butter, divided
1/4 cup	light brown sugar
2 large	pears, peeled, quartered and cored
1 1/8 cups	all-purpose flour
3/4 teaspoon	baking powder
3/4 teaspoon	baking soda
1/2 teaspoon	ground cinnamon
1/2 teaspoon	ground nutmeg
1/4 teaspoon	ground ginger
1/4 teaspoon	salt
1/8 teaspoon	ground allspice
1/2 cup	sugar
1 large	egg
1/3 cup	buttermilk
1/2 teaspoon	vanilla extract
2 tablespoons	molasses

Preheat the oven to 350°F. Melt 2 tablespoons of the butter in a 9-inch round cake pan in the oven. Remove from the oven and sprinkle evenly with the brown sugar. Set aside. Insert the 4mm slicing disc in the Cuisinart® Food Processor. Stand the pear quarters upright in the large feed tube and slice using light pressure. Arrange the slices in the baking pan, fanning them in a circle. Place small pieces of pear in the center.

Combine the flour and next 7 ingredients (baking powder through allspice) in a small bowl and set aside. Wipe the work bowl dry and insert the metal blade. Process the remaining butter and sugar until smooth, about 25 to 30 seconds. Scrape the bowl. Add the egg, buttermilk, vanilla extract and molasses and process 30 seconds to combine. Scrape the work bowl and add the dry ingredients. Pulse just until incorporated, about 5 times. Spread the batter evenly over the pears. Bake until a toothpick inserted in the center comes out clean, about 45 minutes. Cool in the pan on a wire rack. Unmold onto a plate and serve warm.

Makes 8 servings.

Tip: Purchase pears that are firm, but not hard. If necessary, ripen them slightly by placing them in a paper bag and storing at room temperature for 2 to 3 days. Pears are ripe when they are still slightly firm.

Autumn Adventure

When summer ends and the air is just beginning to turn crisp, organize a trip to a nearby pick-your-own apple orchard, farmer's market or to a wooded park to see the glory of autumn and to enjoy a bountiful harvest.

A Frolic in Fall Call

- Affix your invitation to a packet of dried apple slices.
- Attach a small pinecone to ribbon and affix to your heavyweight invitation card stock and send in a small box.
- Type your invitation on a blank label and affix it to a brochure from the apple orchard or park you're visiting.

Picnic Pack-ups

- Load a picnic basket with food (see tips for transporting hot food in Chapter 2), wood-handled flatware, salt and pepper shakers, earthenware bowls, beverage glasses and mugs for your post-picking picnic. Don't forget a sharp knife for cutting cheese wedges and apples.
- Remember to bring a picnic blanket or fall-colored tablecloth for dining.
- Fall foliage-design napkins will add seasonal charm to your spread.
- If it's a long drive, remember to pack snacks for your trip.

Trip Trophies for Holiday Décor

- Collect autumn leaves, gourds, Indian corn and pinecones for decorating.
- Pick apples for making candy apples for Halloween and baking Thanksgiving pies.
- Dry apple slices to be used for creating garlands for autumn and Christmas décor.
- Paint pinecones, or leave natural, to add either sparkle or country charm to your holiday decorations. (However, never burn pinecones in a fireplace. They can explode and, if painted, can release toxic fumes.)

FALL FROLIC FOODS
(Highlighted recipes are included.)

Ratatouille (see tips for transporting hot food in Chapter 2)

Italian Flatbread

Freshly harvested Apples

Blocks or small wheels of Cheddar Cheese

Fresh apple cider, crisp white wine (don't forget the corkscrew) or beverage of choice

Ratatouille — page 53

Ratatouille

1 1/2 pounds	Italian eggplant, cut into 1-inch cubes
2 teaspoons	salt, divided
3 tablespoons	extra virgin olive oil, divided
3/4 pound	zucchini squash, cut into 1-inch cubes
3/4 pound	yellow squash, cut into 1-inch cubes
2 large	yellow onions, peeled, chopped
6 large	cloves garlic, peeled and minced
1 (12 ounce)	fennel bulb, trimmed, fronds reserved, cut in 1/2-inch thick slices
1 large	red bell pepper, cored, seeded and cut in 1-inch pieces
1 large	green bell pepper, cored, seeded, cut in 1-inch pieces
1 tablespoon	herbs de Provence
3 15-ounce	cans recipe-ready diced tomatoes
2 tablespoons	tomato paste
1	bay leaf
1/4 to 1/2 cup	basil leaves, shredded, optional (do not shred until ready to add)

Place the eggplant in a colander and toss with 1 teaspoon of the salt. Let stand for 30 to 60 minutes to allow the salt to draw the bitter flavor from the eggplant. Rinse and dry the eggplant before continuing. Preheat the oven to 325°F.

Heat 1 tablespoon of the olive oil in the Cuisinart® 12-inch Skillet over medium-high heat. Add the drained and dried eggplant cubes. Cook until lightly browned, 5 to 6 minutes. Remove and reserve. Add another tablespoon of the olive oil to the pan. When hot, add the zucchini and yellow squash cubes; cook until lightly browned, 4 to 5 minutes. Remove and reserve.

Heat the last tablespoon of olive oil and add the onions and garlic. Cook the vegetables until softened, but not browned, 4 to 5 minutes. Stir in the sliced fennel, red and green peppers, and herbs de Provence. Cook for 2 to 3 minutes, then stir in the reserved eggplant and squash, along with any accumulated juices. Stir in the tomatoes with juices, tomato paste and bay leaf. Bring the mixture to a simmer. Cover the skillet and place in the preheated oven. Cook for 1 1/2 hours, covered, until the vegetables are tender. Remove the cover, stir and cook for an additional 30 to 40 minutes. Remove the bay leaf and stir in the shredded basil leaves. Garnish with the reserved fennel fronds. Serve hot, warm or cold.

Makes 12 to 16 servings.

Italian Flat Bread

1/3 cup	warm water (105°F to 115°F)
1/4	ounce package active dry yeast
3/4 teaspoon	sugar
4 cups	all-purpose flour
1 1/2 teaspoons	salt
1 cup	cold water
2 tablespoons	vegetable oil
1 small	onion, peeled, ends cut flat
2 small cloves	garlic, peeled
1/2 cup	extra virgin olive oil
1 tablespoon	poppy seeds
1 1/2 teaspoons	red pepper flakes
1 1/4 teaspoons	kosher salt
1/2 teaspoon	ground black pepper
	cooking spray
	cornmeal

Pour the warm water into a 2-cup liquid measuring cup and add the yeast and sugar. Stir to blend well and let stand until foamy, about 3 to 5 minutes. Fit the dough blade on the Cuisinart® Food Processor and place the flour and salt in the work bowl. Add the cold water and oil to the yeast mixture and, with the Food Processor running, pour the oil through the small feed tube as fast as the flour will absorb it. Process until the dough cleans the side of the work bowl and forms a ball, about 40 seconds. Continue processing for 40 seconds, or until the dough is uniformly moist and elastic.

Transfer the dough to a lightly floured large food storage bag. Squeeze the air out of the bag and seal tightly. Let rise in a warm place until doubled in size, about 45 minutes to 1 hour.

Insert the 2mm slicing disc into the Food Processor. Place the onion, cut side down, on the disc and slice using firm pressure. Separate the slices into rings and reserve. Insert the metal blade and process the garlic until finely chopped, about 10 seconds. Scrape the bowl. Add the oil, poppy seeds, red pepper flakes, salt and pepper and process until combined, about 5 seconds.

Preheat the oven to 450°F. Coat 2 baking sheets with the cooking spray and sprinkle with cornmeal. Punch down the dough with lightly floured hands and stretch the dough gently into a freeform rectangle about 10 x 14 inches. With a rolling pin, roll the dough into a rectangle about 12 x 24 inches and about one-fourth inch thick. Cut the rectangle in half. Place each half on a prepared baking sheet and prick with a fork. Brush each flat bread with the oil mixture and top with the onion rings. Bake until golden and crisp, about 10 to 15 minutes. Allow to cool slightly. Use a sharp knife or pizza cutter to slice bread into elongated triangular pieces (or any shape you prefer).

Makes 8 to 10 servings.

Tip: After the dough is punched down it may be refrigerated overnight. If refrigerated, let it stand at room temperature for 20 minutes before rolling.

Italian Flat Bread — page 54

A Winning Super Bowl Party

It doesn't matter if the home team is playing or not, the Super Bowl is one of the biggest party days of the year. So whether your feelings about football are "go-team-go" or not, rally the troops to your pigskin party. Everyone can cheer for this gathering.

Invitations That Score

- Use clip art or design your own football shape with construction paper and use as the base for your party information.
- With clip art or your own design, print your invitations on white heavyweight stock to resemble tickets to the big game.

Stadium Setting

- Use white chalk or washable paint to create yard lines from your driveway to your door.
- Use a hot glue gun to affix a football trading card or a tiny toy football to a ponytail holder. Use as a napkin ring for grab-and-go guests.
- Stand pom-poms in the teams' colors in a megaphone as your buffet table centerpiece.
- Serve chips and/or crackers in football helmet-shaped bowls.

Fan Fun

- Hang a hoop outdoors or in a doorway and have guests test their aim with a foam football during slow game periods or half time.
- Ask guests to choose a team to root for, or have them pick a team from a drawing. Award prizes for those guests whose team is leading at the end of each quarter and/or the game.
- Play a lively game of football trivia for prizes.
- Designate team fans with stickers, temporary tattoos or press-on patches placed onto each guest's sleeve or hand.

FOOTBALL FARE

(Highlighted recipes are included.)

Herbed Goat Cheese Spread served with stone-wheat crackers

Olive Bread

Assorted Chips and Dips

Chili with Black Beans

Seasonal fruit

Herbed Goat Cheese Spread

1 small clove	garlic, peeled
2 tablespoons	fresh herbs, washed and dried*
8 ounces	lowfat cream cheese, cut into 1-inch pieces
4 ounces	goat cheese, cut into 1-inch pieces
1/2 teaspoon	coarsely ground black pepper
1/4 teaspoon	bottled hot sauce
1/8 teaspoon	salt

Fit the Cuisinart® Food Processor with the metal blade and process the garlic and herbs until finely chopped, about 10 seconds. Scrape the bowl. Add the remaining ingredients and process for 10 seconds. Scrape the bowl and process for about 15 seconds until well blended. Chill until ready to serve. Serve with assorted crackers and flat breads.

Makes 1 cup.

*We recommend using a combination of fresh parsley, basil and dill.

Tip: Goat cheese, or chevre cheese, is available in the specialty cheese section of most supermarkets. Chevre is the French word for "goat."

Chili with Black Beans

2 tablespoons	extra virgin olive oil, divided
1 1/2 pounds	lean ground beef
3/4 pound	lean ground pork
2 cups	yellow onion, chopped
4 large cloves	garlic, peeled and minced
1 cup	green pepper, chopped
1/4 cup	jalapeño pepper, finely chopped
3 tablespoons	chili powder
1 teaspoon	ground oregano
28-ounce	can recipe-ready diced tomatoes with juices
1 tablespoon	tomato paste
1	chipotle chile pepper in adobo sauce, chopped*
1 teaspoon	adobo sauce*
2 cups	beef stock or broth
15-ounce	can black beans, drained, rinsed and drained again
2 tablespoons	corn meal or masa harina

Heat half of the olive oil over medium-high heat in the Cuisinart® 8 Quart Stock Pot until it covers the bottom of the pan and is shimmering. Add half the ground beef in large chunks, and let cook without turning until nicely browned, about 3 to 4 minutes. Turn and brown on the other side. Transfer to a plate and repeat with the remaining beef; then the ground pork. Pour off and discard the grease. Reduce the heat to low and add the remaining olive oil. Add the onion and garlic. Cook until the vegetables are softened and translucent. Add the peppers, chili powder and oregano. Sauté for 4 to 5 minutes, until the peppers begin to soften and the spices are fragrant. Stir in the reserved browned meats, tomatoes with juices, tomato paste, chipotle chile with sauce and salt. Increase the heat to high, add the stock and bring to a boil. Reduce the heat to low, cover loosely and simmer over low heat for 1 1/2 to 2 hours, stirring occasionally. Stir in the black beans and corn meal. Simmer uncovered for an additional 20 to 30 minutes. Serve with a garnish of shredded cheddar cheese and sour cream.

Makes 10 cups.

> Recipe Notes:*Chipotle chiles in adobo sauce are available in cans in the ethnic foods section of most grocery stores. A chipotle chile pepper is a dried smoked jalapeño with a unique smoky, yet sweet, somewhat chocolaty flavor. The chipotle is a hot chile and a small amount goes a long way. The flavor it provides is distinctive and integral to this recipe. Unused portions may be frozen.

Chili is actually best when made a day ahead. Stop the cooking process before adding the beans and corn meal. Cool, cover and refrigerate. When cold, remove any visible fat that has congealed. Reheat and continue as the recipe directs.

Shower the Bride

When it's time to host a bridal shower, keep the bride's interests, heritage, hobbies, talents or wedding colors in mind for use with planning a theme. In this case, we've selected a high tea as the theme and the varying hues of purple as the décor colors.

Shower Summons

- Write the invitation on hand-made paper pressed with lavender-colored flower petals (available at arts and crafts or stationery stores).
- Enclose a tea bag or affix one to your heavyweight invitation card stock to help set the high tea style.
- Create an invitation of your own design, or use clip art, to fashion the invitation in the shape of a teapot or teacup.
- Advise the guests where the bridal couple is registered for their gifts.

Shower Setting

- Arrange purple hydrangeas and lilacs in floral teapots and display violets in floral teacups as centerpieces and general party décor.
- Drape a lavender floral to-the-floor cloth on your buffet.
- Tie lavender ribbons to the backs of each guest's chair and affix a nosegay of small purple flowers for décor and a gift-to-go.
- Attach a purple floral garland to the frame of a high-backed, white wicker chair for your guest of honor.

Shower Playtime

- Divide the guests into teams of two. Give each team a roll of white toilet tissue, clear tape, and straight pins. Instruct one team member to create a toilet tissue wedding gown on the other team member in a fixed period of time. Let the bride-to-be judge the best "gown" and award prizes to the winning duo.

- Pass around a decorative journal or autograph book in which each guest inscribes a wish or a piece of advice for the guest of honor. Instant photos of guests can be added to the page near their wishes to complete this tea time treasure.

Shower Souvenirs

- Individual floral teapots
- Teacups planted with African violets
- Nosegays affixed to the chairs

TEMPTING TEAS AND TASTES
(Highlighted recipes are included.)

Serve the ladies their choice of teas in individual teapots
that they can keep as a shower favor.

Stack petit fours on a tiered cake plate and garnish with edible pansies.

Roll out a **Lemon Sponge Cake with Raspberry Sauce** on a flower-draped tea cart to serve as your showpiece dessert.

Lemon Sponge Cake with Raspberry Sauce

	cooking spray
I cup	cake flour
2 teaspoons	baking powder
1/2 cup	lowfat buttermilk
I tablespoon	butter
8 strips	lemon zest, cut in half*
2/3 cup	sugar
I large	egg

Preheat the oven to 350°F. Coat an 8-inch cake pan with cooking spray. Combine the cake flour and baking powder in a small bowl and set aside. Place the buttermilk and butter in a 1-cup liquid measuring cup. Heat in a microwave oven until the butter is almost melted, about 1 1/2 minutes on 70% power. Set aside.

Fit the Cuisinart® Food Processor with the metal blade and process the zest and sugar until finely chopped, about 1 minute. Add the egg and process 1 minute. Scrape the bowl and process 1 minute. While the Food Processor is running, pour the milk mixture through the feed tube and process until combined, about 10 seconds. Scrape the bowl. Add the dry ingredients and pulse until just combined, about 3 to 4 times. Pour the batter into the prepared pan and bake until the top is lightly browned and springs back when touched, about 20 minutes.

Cool the cake in the pan on a wire rack for 10 minutes. Remove the cake from the pan and cool completely. Cut the cake into 8 pieces and slice each piece in half horizontally with a serrated knife. Place the bottom half of the cake on a dessert plate and drizzle 1 tablespoon raspberry sauce over the half. Top with other half of cake and drizzle 1 tablespoon of sauce over the top of the cake. Garnish with whipped cream and fresh raspberries, if desired. Serve immediately.

Makes 8 servings.

* Use a vegetable peeler to remove the zest from the lemons.
The "zest" is the colorful outer part of the skin. Do not use the bitter white pith.

Tip: Cake flour is used to make tender baked goods. It is available in the baking
section of most supermarkets. To substitute all-purpose flour for cake flour,
measure out 1 cup all-purpose flour and remove 2 tablespoons.

Raspberry Sauce

12 ounces	**frozen raspberries, thawed**
2 tablespoons	**superfine sugar**
1 tablespoon	**lemon juice**

Fit the Cuisinart® Food Processor with the metal blade and process the raspberries, sugar and lemon juice until combined, about 10 seconds. Place a fine mesh strainer in a small mixing bowl and pour the raspberry sauce into the strainer. Stir with a spoon until the sauce has passed through the strainer. Discard the seeds. Use the sauce as directed above.

Makes 1 cup.

Tip: The sauce may be made ahead and stored in an airtight container
in the refrigerator until ready to use.

Showering New Parents and Baby with Love

A shower is a lovely way for guests to share their joy with the mom or parents-to-be. Showers can be coed or simply for the mom. (With the parents' permission, share the gender of the child with the guests so they can select gifts accordingly.)

It's also easy to select a sweet theme. Simply choose cartoon or fairy tale characters, nursery rhymes, colors, the alphabet, children's books or anything else you believe the expectant parent(s) and your guests would enjoy. In fact, if you know the décor the parents intend to use for the baby's room, it can be the ideal theme.

This shower scheme is designed with a circus theme and primary colors.

Come to the Circus

- Use clip art forms or your own creation to fashion an invitation in the shape or design of a circus tent.
- Enclose your printed invitation inside a new paper peanut or popcorn bag.
- Find a lion's image and headline the caption, "(Parents' names) are roaring with delight over the impending birth of their baby" and the party particulars.
- For a surprise shower, cut out an elephant's shape and add the caption, "Don't forget…it's a surprise" to your invitation details.

Under the Big Top

- Drape long strands of red crepe paper or wide red ribbon from the center of the party room's ceiling and down the walls around the room to give the illusion of a circus big top.
- Cover your buffet table in a primary color or red and white striped cloth.
- Use painted boxes or a child's train set to make up a circus train as a table decoration.

Send in the Clowns

- Ask each guest to bring their baby photo. Mount the photos on a board and assign each a number. Then ask guests to match up each baby photo with an attendee. The one who guesses the most correctly wins a prize. (Have multiple prizes in case more than one guest wins.)

Sideshow Souvenirs

- Boxes of animal crackers
- Decorative tins of gourmet popcorn

CONCESSION CUISINE
(Highlighted recipes are included.)

Rent a popcorn and/or cotton candy machine.

Serve beverages with striped straws.

Ice Cream Sundaes with Toasted Almond Ice Cream and
Mocha Chip Ice Cream

Mocha Chip Ice Cream

I cup	whole milk, well-chilled
3/4 cup	granulated sugar
2 tablespoons	instant espresso powder
2 tablespoons	unsweetened cocoa powder
2 cups	heavy cream, well-chilled
2 teaspoons	pure vanilla extract
1/2 cup	mini chocolate morsels

In a medium bowl, use the Cuisinart® Hand Mixer at Low speed to combine the milk, sugar, espresso powder and cocoa until dissolved, about 1 to 2 minutes. Add the heavy cream and vanilla and blend well.

Assemble the Cuisinart® Automatic Frozen Yogurt – Ice Cream & Sorbet Maker. The chiller bowl should be totally frozen before use. Turn the machine to On and pour the milk and sugar into the freezer bowl. Mix until thickened, about 25 to 30 minutes. Add the chocolate morsels to the ice cream during the last 5 minutes of freezing. Turn the machine to Off. The ice cream will have a soft texture. If desired, transfer the ice cream to an airtight container and freeze for 2 hours until firm. If frozen, let the ice cream stand at room temperature for 10 minutes prior to serving.

Makes 10 1/2-cup servings.

A Family and Friends Reunion

The arrival of visiting friends or relatives is the perfect time to organize a reunion. Or, gather the gang if you haven't been together for a while. For additional fun, select a theme for the occasion. In this plan, we've chosen to use photos as the theme.

Picture-Perfect Invitations

- Select a photo of the guest(s) of honor, preferably at a past celebration. Or, create a collage of photos of your intended guests. Add the caption, "Picture Yourself at Our Party," along with the party information and duplicate the sheet on a color copier.

- Ask everyone to send along copies of photos to share with the other reunion guests and for use as party decorations.

- Encourage guests to bring duplicates of photos of themselves and other guests for a photo exchange at the reunion. Or, invite them to bring along photo albums so other guests can reminisce with them.

The Photo Gallery

- As each guest arrives with their photo, fasten the photo to a photo "line." Suspend fishing line at eye-level around your walls using staples. Use decorative paper clips or small plastic clothespins to fasten the photos to the line so that your room(s) resembles an art gallery.

Picture the Fun

- Set up a website with the photos that the guests have shared, along with pictures taken at the party. You can also create an online message board for guests to use to keep in touch. If you set up an address book, gather the e-mail address of each guest so you can start a newsletter list.

- Have a number of disposable cameras at the party so that guests can take photos to be duplicated and distributed to everyone. Or, put the best photos onto the reunion website.

- Show videos of past gatherings. You can even leave the sound off so the images provide additional décor, but don't interfere with the guests' conversations. Or, set up a special room where guests can view videos at their leisure.

- For outdoor events in warm weather, set up family-style games such as a three-legged race, a water balloon toss, a tug-of-war and the like to encourage all generations to participate.

- Gather everyone together for a group photograph.

Snapshot Souvenirs

- Small picture frames
- Photo frames imprinted with the date of the reunion to hold the group picture taken at the party

FAVORITE FAMILY FARE
(Highlighted recipes are included.)

Assorted cheeses and fresh vegetable crudites

**Caramelized Onions with Roasted Red Pepper
and Sherry Vinegar on Bruschetta**

Beef Stew for a Crowd

Hot rolls

Beef Stew for a Crowd — page 68

Carmelized Onions with Roasted Red Pepper and Sherry Vinegar on Bruschetta

For the Caramelized Onions:

3 to 4 cloves	garlic, peeled and finely chopped *
2 pounds	Spanish onions, peeled, cut in quarters vertically, then sliced about 1/8-inch thick *
1 tablespoon	unsalted butter
1 tablespoon	extra virgin olive oil
1 teaspoon	herbs de Provence
2	roasted red peppers, cut in 1" x 1/4" julienne strips
1/2 teaspoon	salt
1 tablespoon	sherry wine vinegar
2 ounces	Asiago or Manchego cheese, shaved

For the Grilled Bruschetta:

1 pound	crusty baguette (about 24 inches)
1/2 cup	extra virgin olive oil
2 cloves	garlic, peeled and halved

To make the caramelized onions, melt the butter with the olive oil over medium-high heat in a Cuisinart® 12-inch Skillet (regular or nonstick finish). When the butter is bubbling, add the chopped onions and garlic. Stir to coat completely with the butter/oil mixture. Reduce the heat to medium and cook the onion and garlic for about 20 minutes, stirring occasionally. Sprinkle the herbs de Provence over the onion and let soften and become aromatic. Continue caramelizing the onions for another 10 to 15 minutes, until they begin to turn golden. Stir in the roasted peppers and salt. Cook for another 5 minutes. Stir in the sherry vinegar and cook until the vinegar is completely reduced, about 5 minutes.

Makes 3 cups.

To prepare the bruschetta, cut the bread into slices about 1/4 to 1/3-inch thick. Brush both sides of each slice lightly with olive oil. Heat the Cuisinart® 12-inch Skillet over medium-high heat. Sauté the slices about 1 1/2 to 2 minutes on each side, or until golden brown and crisp outside, but still soft inside. Rub the toasts with garlic on one side. The toasts may be made 1 week ahead and kept in an airtight container. Makes about 40 pieces of toast.

To serve: Spoon about 1 to 1 1/2-tablespoons of the caramelized onions onto each slice of the toast, and top with a scant sprinkling of shredded cheese. Warm for 1 to 2 minutes under the broiler or serve at room temperature.

Makes about 40 bruschetta.

*Using the Cuisinart® Food Processor makes the chopping and slicing steps simple. Insert the metal blade and, with the food processor running, drop the garlic through the small feed tube and process 10 seconds to chop. Leave the garlic in the work bowl. Replace the blade with the 3 or 4 mm slicing disc and slice the onions. You will have about 12 cups sliced onions.

Carmelized Onions with Roasted Red Pepper and Sherry Vinegar on Bruschetta

Beef Stew for a Crowd

4 pounds	**beef chuck (yields 3 1/4 to 3 1/2 pounds when trimmed)**
1 1/2 pounds	**baby carrots, peeled, cut in half**
1 pound	**button mushrooms, cleaned, cut into 1-inch pieces if large**
1 pound	**new white or red potatoes, cut into 1/2-inch pieces**
1 large (8 ounce)	**onion, peeled and cut in 1/2-inch pieces**
1	**red bell pepper, cored, seeded and cut in 1/2-inch pieces**
12 cloves	**garlic, peeled**
2 14.5-ounce	**cans recipe-ready diced tomatoes with juices**
1 cup	**fresh bread crumbs made from crusty bread**
1/4 cup	**instant tapioca**
1 tablespoon	**herbs de Provence***
1	**bay leaf**
1/2 teaspoon	**salt**
1/2 teaspoon	**freshly ground black pepper**
1 1/2 cups	**dry red wine (use a good wine that has depth and quality)**
1 cup	**fat free, low sodium beef stock or broth**
1/2 pound	**pearl onions, peeled and blanched (you may substitute frozen, thawed)**
2 cups	**green peas (you may substitute frozen, thawed)**
1/4 cup	**Italian parsley, chopped**

Arrange the oven rack in the lower third of the oven. Preheat the oven to 325°F. Trim the beef chuck of any visible fat and gristle and cut into 1/2-inch cubes. Place the beef cubes, carrots, mushrooms, potatoes, onion, red bell pepper, garlic, tomatoes with juices, bread crumbs, instant tapioca, herbs, bay leaf, salt and pepper in a large bowl. Stir to combine. Transfer the stew to a Cuisinart® 8 Quart Stock Pot. Add the wine and beef stock to the pot. Cover and place in the oven for 4 hours. Do not open the oven while the stew is cooking. After 4 hours, add the pearl onions and green peas. Let the stew remain in the oven for an additional 15 minutes, uncovered. Stir in the chopped parsley and serve hot.

Makes 12 servings.

---

*You may change the flavor of the stew by changing the herbs. Try using an Italian herb blend or a Southwestern herb blend.

Chapter 5

Celebrating the Holidays

Valentine's Day Sweetheart Supper

Unplug your phones and take a night off from everyday pressures to concentrate on love and each other. Let us play Cupid to help you set the stage for a romantic rendezvous with your sweetheart on Valentine's Day.

A Sexy Summons

- Leave a heart-shaped note on his pillow, in his briefcase, or in his shaving kit inviting him to your tête-à-tête.

- Give him a note inside an empty, heart-shaped candy box and tell him that if he wants something sweet, you'll be waiting for him that night.

Building a Love Nest for Two

- Clear the clutter or anything else (bills, laundry, exercise equipment and so on) that might detract or distract you from your romantic evening.

- Your table can be set up in your dining room, or on your terrace in warmer climates. For a more intimate setting, put a small dining table and chairs in your bedroom.

- Dim the lights, add lower-wattage light bulbs, or drape a scarf over your lamps to give the room a soft glow.

- Light up your home with candles. (For safety's sake, never leave a burning candle unattended.)

- Cover your table with a to-the-floor white lace tablecloth or with a red or soft pink cloth.

- Scatter rose petals, heart-shaped confetti or candy hearts on your table.
- Use your best china, flatware and crystal to serve dinner.
- Play romantic music (possibly even your wedding song) to accompany dinner.
- If he's given you flowers, set them on the table. (With a tall arrangement, set the vase a little off-center so that it won't block your view of each other.)

A RECIPE FOR ROMANCE
(Highlighted recipes are included.)

Clear Consommé

Shrimp and Tomatoes À la Grecque

Fluffy White Rice

Fresh Green Beans with Water Chestnuts

Zabaglione with Fresh Mixed Berries

White wine or champagne

Shrimp and Tomatoes À la Grecque

2 teaspoons	extra virgin olive oil
I to 2 cloves	garlic, peeled and chopped
I large	shallot, peeled and chopped
I teaspoon	ground oregano
1/4 cup	dry white vermouth
15 1/2 ounce	can recipe-ready diced tomatoes
1/4 teaspoon	salt
1/8 teaspoon	freshly ground black pepper
I 1/2 pounds	fresh shrimp (16 – 20 count), peeled and deveined
1/4 cup	crumbled feta cheese (about I ounce)
1/4 cup	Italian parsley, chopped

Heat the olive oil in a Cuisinart® 10-inch Skillet over medium heat. When hot, add the garlic, shallot and oregano. Cook, stirring, for 2 to 3 minutes until softened and translucent. Add the vermouth and cook to reduce by half, another 2 to 3 minutes. Stir in the tomatoes with their juices, salt and pepper. Simmer for 5 to 6 minutes until slightly thickened. Add the shrimp and cook, stirring occasionally until firm and pink, but not overcooked. Remove from the heat. Sprinkle the shrimp with feta and parsley. Serve hot.

Makes 4 servings.

Zabaglione with Fresh Mixed Berries

8 large	egg yolks
1/2 cup	sugar
1/2 cup	dry white wine
1/2 cup	Framboise, Chambord, Kirschwasser or Triple Sec
3 pints	mixed fresh berries, washed, dried, and sliced if large

Place the egg yolks and sugar in a Cuisinart® Double Boiler. Whisk until the sauce reaches a creamy consistency. In the bottom pan of the double boiler, bring a small amount of water to a simmer and continue to whisk over the simmering water until the sauce is thick and pale yellow. Add the wine and liqueur, whisking rapidly until well incorporated. Continue to whisk over the simmering water until the mixture is thickened and fluffy, about 4 to 6 minutes. Remove from the heat.

If desired, place the berries in a serving bowl or individual serving bowls. Spoon the zabaglione over the berries and serve. Place the berries in an oven-proof gratin dish, top with the zabaglione and place under the broiler or use a butane torch to brown lightly. Serve immediately.

Makes 8 servings.

Note: For easiest whisking, use a Cuisinart® 7 Speed SmartPower™ Electronic Hand Mixer fitted with the Professional Chef's Whisk.

St. Patrick's Day Pub Setting

An Irish Invitation

- Pen your invitation on the petals of a paper shamrock.
- Type your invitation details on a plain label and affix to a small package of Lucky Charms® cereal.
- Use clip art or draw your own rainbow. Write your invitation information on the rainbow's bands.
- Encourage guests to come dressed in green.

The Setting

- Line your walkway with pots of shamrocks or clover.
- For a more elegant approach, drape a lace overlay over your green tablecloth.
- Another fun approach is to cut out oversized shamrocks from green poster board to use as placemats.
- Rim the table's edge with rainbow-colored ribbon pinned to your tablecloth.
- String a rainbow of balloons over your buffet table, or attach it to your walls.
- Recycle a black witch's cauldron from Halloween for use as a centerpiece. Fill it with gold-colored plastic or chocolate coins. Prop up a toy leprechaun next to the pot.
- Tie the handles of beer mugs with green or rainbow-colored ribbons.

An Irish Fling

- Like any good Irish pub, be sure yours has a dartboard or two.

SHAMROCK SPREAD

(Highlighted recipes are included.)

Guinness-Braised Bratwurst Hoagies

Roasted Potato Wedges

Chilled Cole Slaw with Caraway seeds

Pints of Guinness beer

Guinness-Braised Bratwurst Hoagies

1/4 cup	butter
2	yellow onions, thinly sliced
1 teaspoon	ground black pepper
2 pounds	bratwurst (about 8 links)
3 12-ounce	cans Guinness beer
8	hoagie rolls, split
1/4 cup	prepared grainy mustard

In the Cuisinart® 12-inch Skillet, melt the butter over medium heat. Add the onions and the black pepper to the melted butter and cook for five minutes. Add the sausages to the skillet and cook for another 5 to 10 minutes, or until the bratwurst is lightly browned. Add the Guinness beer to the skillet and bring the liquid to a simmer. Reduce the heat to low and simmer for 20 minutes.

To serve, spread each hoagie roll lightly with the grainy mustard. Place the sausages equally in the hoagie rolls and top the sausages with the grilled onions.

Makes 8 servings.

Easter or Passover Brunch for the Bunch

When tulips and crocuses poke their heads from the cold winter's earth, you know that Spring is just around the corner. One of the earliest springtime holidays you'll celebrate will be Easter or Passover. These joyful celebrations also herald a season of warm weather entertaining opportunities. Here is a Spring brunch your guests will enjoy.

Come to Our Spring Fling

- Write your invitation on a label and attach it to a flower or vegetable seed packet.
- Pen your party information on floral bordered invitation stock.
- Use clip art, or create your own design, and write your party particulars on the petals of a flower.
- Use a hot glue gun to affix a tiny silk blossom to your heavyweight invitation card stock.

Geared to a Garden

- Line your walkway with potted flowers.
- Drape your table with a floral or pastel-colored cloth.
- Tie the backs of your chairs with pastel-colored ribbons or a silk floral garland.
- Bend the wire stems of silk flowers and wrap them around your rolled pastel or floral napkins.
- Tie a bow on your stemware glasses with a pastel-colored ribbon.
- Use a paint pen to write your guests' names on individual terracotta pots that contain flowers or fresh herbs for triple use as a place card, decoration and a gift-to-go.
- Finely chop colorful vegetables and herbs to sprinkle like edible confetti on the rims of your plates.
- Wrap the handle of a basket with ribbons or silk flowers. Use it to serve matzos for Passover or bread and rolls for Easter.

Holiday Fun

- Stage an Easter egg hunt. For indoor events, use plastic eggs filled with age-appropriate trinkets.

Seasonal Souvenirs

- Flower or vegetable seed packets
- Potted plants used as the place cards
- Gardening tools
- Decorative watering cans

BRUNCH FOR YOUR BUNCH

(Highlighted recipes are included.)

Mango Frosty

Creamy Tomato-Basil Soup

Bread and rolls (for Easter)

Matzos (for Passover)

Asparagus, Mushroom & Smoked Gouda Omelet

Apple Almond Waffles

Orange slices or other fresh fruit

Coffee or tea

Creamy Tomato-Basil Soup

I small clove	garlic, peeled
1/4 cup	fresh basil leaves, washed and dried
1 1/2 cups	low sodium tomato juice
1/2 cup	reduced-sodium, lowfat chicken broth
1 cup	plain nonfat yogurt
3/4 pound	ripe tomatoes, cored, cut into 1/2-inch pieces
1/8 teaspoon	finely ground black pepper

Place the garlic and basil in the Cuisinart® SmartPower™ 7-Speed Electronic Blender jar and cover. Pulse on Stir until coarsely chopped, about 5 to 6 times. Scrape the jar, if necessary. Add the remaining ingredients in the order listed and blend on Purée until combined, about 30 to 35 seconds. Pour the soup into a large bowl. Cover and chill until ready to serve.

Makes six 6-ounce servings.

Tip: For best flavor, select tomatoes that are firm and richly colored. Always store tomatoes at room temperature. Never place them in the refrigerator.

Creamy Tomato-Basil Soup

Asparagus, Mushroom & Smoked Gouda Omelet

2 large	eggs
2 large	egg whites
1/8 teaspoon	salt
1/8 teaspoon	freshly ground black pepper
4 stalks	asparagus, trimmed, peeled, cut into 3/4-inch lengths
3	crimini mushrooms, cleaned and sliced
1	plum tomato, cored and sliced
1 teaspoon	unsalted butter, divided
2 tablespoons	smoked Gouda, shredded (about 1/2-ounce)
1 tablespoon	chives, chopped

Place the eggs and egg whites in a medium bowl. Blend with a whisk until combined. Add the salt and pepper. Reserve.

Place the asparagus in a Cuisinart® 8-inch Skillet and cover with water. Bring to a boil over high heat and cook the asparagus for 1 to 2 minutes, until crisp tender or cooked to taste. Drain and reserve.

Melt half the butter in the skillet over medium-high heat. Add the mushrooms and sauté 2 to 3 minutes, until lightly browned on both sides. Add half the tomato slices and cook until heated through, about 1 to 2 minutes. Remove and reserve. Melt the remaining 1/2-teaspoon of butter in the skillet over medium heat. Add the egg mixture. When the eggs begin to set, push the edges back, allowing the uncooked egg to flow underneath. When the bottom of the omelet is lightly browned and the top is nearly set, sprinkle evenly with the cheese and half of the chopped chives. Top with the asparagus, mushrooms and tomatoes. Fold one side of the omelet over the filling and roll out onto a warmed plate. Arrange the remaining tomato slices on the omelet and sprinkle with the remaining chives. Garnish with avocado slices, if desired.

Makes 1 entrée serving.

Recipe note: We have substituted 2 egg whites for 1 whole egg.
If you wish, you may use 3 whole eggs.

Apple Almond Waffles

1 1/4 cups	all-purpose flour
3/4 cup	whole wheat flour
1/2 cup	almonds, chopped
3 tablespoons	packed brown sugar
1 tablespoon	baking powder
1 teaspoon	ground cinnamon
1/2 teaspoon	ground ginger
1/2 teaspoon	baking soda
1/2 teaspoon	salt
1 1/2 cups	reduced fat milk
2 large	eggs, lightly beaten
6 tablespoons	unsalted butter, melted and cooled
2/3 cup	tart apple, shredded

Place the flours and almonds in a large mixing bowl. Crumble the brown sugar to remove any lumps and add along with the baking powder, cinnamon, ginger, baking soda and salt. Stir to blend. Add the milk, eggs, butter and shredded apple. Stir to combine until well-blended. Let the batter rest 5 minutes before using. Preheat your Cuisinart® Heart Shaped Waffle Maker on Setting #3* (The green indicator light will be illuminated when preheated.)

Pour 1/3 cup batter onto the center of the lower grid. Use a heatproof spatula to spread the batter to within 1/2-inch of the edge of the grid. Close the lid of the waffle maker. The indicator light will turn red. When the light turns green again, the waffle is ready. Open the lid and carefully remove the baked waffle. Repeat with the remaining batter. For best results, serve immediately. You may keep the waffles warm until ready to serve on a wire rack placed on a baking sheet in a 200°F oven.

Makes 10 6-inch round heart waffles.

*We recommend using setting #3 to achieve a golden brown baked waffle.
Adjust the browning control if you prefer lighter or darker waffles.*

A Traditional Thanksgiving to Treasure

Join Us to Give Thanks

- Cut out an autumn leaf shape you traced on gold, burnt orange or light brown construction paper. Print your invitation on the leaf.
- Type your invitation on a plain label and affix it to a packet of turkey gravy mix.
- Write out your favorite pumpkin pie recipe on fall-colored paper and add your invitation to the back of the recipe.

Decking the Hall for Fall

- Line your walkway with potted mums and/or pumpkins.
- Drape your table with a gold, burnt orange, russet, forest green or burgundy cloth.
- Loosely arrange fall leaves, gourds, pinecones and apples down the center of your table as a free-flowing centerpiece. (If you're concerned about sap from the fresh foliage staining your cloth, cover the area with clear plastic before setting up your arrangement.)
- Use a paint pen to write the name of each guest on a real or ceramic mini pumpkin or gourd. This will serve as a place card, décor and guest gift.
- Tie fall-colored or fall-patterned napkins with raffia.
- Fasten a small sprig of fall leaves (real or preserved) to the backs of each chair with raffia or fall-colored ribbon.

Fall Frolic and Fun

- Set up a touch football game in your yard or air one of the many televised football games played on Thanksgiving.
- Ask each guest to recite one thing for which they are grateful.
- Pull names out of a decorated basket for your annual Christmas/Hanukkah gift exchange.
- If children are part of your Thanksgiving plans, let them create autumn leaf designs for use as coasters and decorations.

Take-home Gifts

- Booklets of favorite family recipes
- Small jugs of fresh cider
- Pots of mums
- Tiny pumpkin or gourd place holders

A BOUNTIFUL SPREAD

(Highlighted recipes are included.)

Tossed Salad with Blue Cheese Dressing

Roast Turkey with Stuffing

Brown & Wild Rices with Dried Cranberries & Toasted Walnuts

Horseradish Mashed Potatoes

Jalapeño Cranberry Relish with Toasted Walnuts

Peas and Pearl Onions

Pumpkin Crème Caramel

Coffee, tea and cold beverages

Brown & Wild Rices with Dried Cranberries & Toasted Walnuts

1 tablespoon	unsalted butter
1/3 cup	shallot or red onion, peeled and chopped
1/4 cup	celery, chopped
1/4 cup	green pepper, chopped
1/2 teaspoon	herbs de Provence
1 cup	brown basmati rice
1/2 cup	wild rice
1 1/2 cups	fat free, salt free chicken or vegetable stock/broth
1 cup	water
1/2 teaspoon	salt
1/8 teaspoon	freshly ground black pepper
1/2 cup	dried cranberries or dried tart cherries, chopped
1/3 cup	toasted walnuts or pecans, chopped
3 tablespoons	green onion, chopped
3 tablespoons	Italian parsley, chopped

Melt the butter in the Cuisinart® 1 1/2 Quart Saucepan over medium heat. Add the shallots, celery, green pepper and herbs de Provence. Sauté over medium heat until the vegetables are softened and herbs are aromatic, about 3 minutes. Stir in the brown and wild rice, stock, water, salt and pepper. Increase the heat and bring to a boil. Reduce the heat, cover tightly and simmer for 45 to 50 minutes until the liquid is completely absorbed. Stir in the dried cranberries, nuts, green onion and parsley. Cover and let rest 3 to 5 minutes before serving. Serve hot.

Makes 6 to 8 servings.

Horseradish Mashed Potatoes

4 pounds	Yukon gold or russet potatoes, peeled, cut in 1/2-inch slices
4 tablespoons	unsalted butter
2 cups	whole milk, heated
2 to 3 tablespoons	horseradish, finely grated
1/2 to 1 teaspoon	salt
1/4 teaspoon	freshly ground pepper (black or white)

Bring 4 quarts salted water to a boil in the Cuisinart® 6 Quart Stockpot over high heat. (For quickest results, cover loosely.) Add the peeled and sliced potatoes, lower the heat to medium, cover loosely and cook until the potatoes are fork tender, about 15 minutes. Drain and return the potatoes to the stockpot. Place the pan over low heat for 1 minute to dry potatoes. Using a Cuisinart® SmartPower™ Hand Mixer fitted with the beaters, mash the potatoes on low speed for 45 to 60 seconds. Add the butter and continue beating until smooth, about 20 to 30 seconds. While beating, add the hot milk, one-half cup at a time, allowing the milk to be absorbed completely before adding the next half cup. For a "mashed" potato texture, continue using a low speed, for a "whipped" potato texture, use medium speed. Add 2 tablespoons of the horseradish and the salt and pepper and continue to beat until the potatoes are completely blended. Taste and adjust the seasonings, adding more horseradish, salt or pepper as necessary.

Makes 12 servings.

Jalapeño Cranberry Relish with Toasted Walnuts

1/2 cup	walnut halves or pieces, shells removed
	zest of 3 oranges, bitter white pith removed
1 cup	sugar
1 to 2	jalapeño peppers, stemmed, seeded and quartered, to taste
4 cups	fresh whole cranberries (may use frozen, unthawed)
1	navel orange, peeled, cut into quarters

Preheat oven to 350°F. Place the walnuts in a baking pan and toast until golden brown and fragrant, about 8 to 10 minutes. Cool slightly.

Insert the metal blade in the Cuisinart® Prep 11 Plus™ Food Processor. Process the zest with 1/4 cup of the sugar until finely chopped, about 45 seconds. Add the cranberries, jalapeños, oranges and toasted walnuts. Pulse until coarsely chopped, about 10 to 12 times.

Add the remaining sugar, pulse 10 times to blend. Pulse several more times if a finer consistency is desired. Allow the relish to sit for 30 minutes for the flavors to blend before serving. Keep the relish refrigerated. This relish may be made up to 5 days in advance and stored in the refrigerator until ready to use

Makes 4 cups.

Pumpkin Crème Caramel

1 1/3 cups	granulated sugar
6	eggs, beaten
1 1/2 cups	canned solid pack pumpkin
12 ounces	evaporated fat-free milk
1/2 cup	light brown sugar, packed
1 teaspoon	ground cinnamon
1/2 teaspoon	ground ginger
1/2 teaspoon	ground allspice
2 teaspoons	orange zest, finely chopped (remove bitter white pith before chopping)
2 teaspoons	vanilla extract

Preheat the oven to 325°F. Prepare 8 clean six-ounce ramekins.

Melt the granulated sugar in the Cuisinart® 12-inch Skillet over medium-high heat, shaking the skillet occasionally. When the sugar starts to melt, reduce heat to low. Cook, stirring frequently with a wooden spoon, until sugar is golden brown. Remove the skillet from the heat. Immediately pour the caramelized sugar into the 8 ungreased six-ounce custard cups. Holding each cup with a potholder, quickly tilt to evenly coat the bottoms of the cups. Place the custard cups in two 9-inch square baking dishes.

Place the eggs, pumpkin, evaporated milk, brown sugar, spices, orange zest and vanilla in the Cuisinart® SmartPower Premier™ Blender jar. Cover and blend for 30 seconds on Low speed. Pour the pumpkin puree through a strainer to remove the foam. Pour the pumpkin puree over the caramelized sugar in the cups. Place the baking dishes on the oven rack. Pour boiling water into the baking dishes to a depth of 1 inch.

Bake for 40 to 45 minutes or until a knife inserted near the center of the custard comes out clean. Remove the cups from the water and cool on a wire rack. Cover and chill for 4 to 24 hours.

To serve, loosen the edges of each custard with a knife, slipping the point of a knife down the side of the cup. Invert a dessert plate over each custard, turn the cup and plate over together. Scrape the caramelized sugar that remains in the cup onto the custard.

Makes 8 servings.

Home for the Holidays

Whether you're celebrating Christmas or Hanukkah, the winter holidays are a time to gather together those you love to share your heart and hearth. The following are a collection of ideas to start your own holiday traditions.

Join Us for the Holidays

- Use a hot glue gun to affix a flat tree ornament to heavyweight card stock for your Christmas invitation. Mail this in a cushioned envelope.
- Cut out a Star of David on blue paper and pen your invitation to your Hanukkah dinner on the star with silver ink.

Decking the Christmas Halls

- While red and green are traditional colors, you can also choose colors that coordinate with your home's design for your holiday table and room décor.
- For your centerpiece, create your own or buy a plain Christmas wreath. Trim the greenery with a battery-operated set of twinkle lights. Nestle tall taper candles in holders, or pillar candles, in the center of the wreath. Adorn the greenery with cinnamon sticks, dried apple slices, small ornaments or whatever embellishments you'd like. (Do not arrange flammable materials near an open flame.)
- Hang a small, personalized stocking on the back of each chair as a decoration, a gift and a place card.
- Hot glue a silk poinsettia blossom to ribbon and use it to tie your napkins. Or, tie napkins with a colorful licorice string for a sweet reminder of Christmas past.

Decorating Your Home for Hanukkah

- Cover your table with a white, silver or blue cloth.
- Set a second Menorah on the center of your table. Circle the Menorah with children's blocks to spell out "Hanukkah."
- Tie a small dreidel to each napkin with a silver or blue ribbon.
- Attach a small bag of gelt to the back of each chair with silver or blue ribbons.

Songs and Stories

- Give out song sheets and lead everyone in singing holiday songs.
- Jewish children will have fun playing with their dreidels or other Hanukkah toys while Christian children will likely want to play with their new Christmas gifts.
- Read the story of the first Christmas or first Hanukkah.

Holiday Take-Homes

- Tree ornaments (Christmas)
- Small Menorah (Hanukkah)
- Dreidels and gelt (Hanukkah)
- Personalized Christmas stockings filled with trinkets or candy (Christmas)

HOLIDAY HELPINGS
(Highlighted recipes are included.)

Arugula and Green Olives with Balsamic Vinaigrette

Beef Tenderloin with **Mushroom & Port Sauce**

Herbed New Potato & Mushroom Pan Roast with Green Beans

Whole Grain Dinner Rolls

Toasted Almond Pear Clafoutis

Red Wine (merlot or cabernet) or a beverage of choice

Beef Tenderloin with Mushroom & Port Sauce — page 86

Mushroom & Port Sauce

1/4 ounce	dried mushrooms, such as porcini (cèpes) or shiitake
1 cup	boiling water
1/2 tablespoon	unsalted butter, at room temperature
1/2 tablespoon	all-purpose flour
2 to 3	crimini mushrooms, cleaned and chopped (1/2 cup)
1/4 cup	shallots, chopped
1 tablespoon	extra virgin olive oil
1/2 teaspoon	dried thyme
1/2 cup	port wine (red or white)
3/4 cup	fat free, low sodium chicken stock/broth
3/4 cup	fat free, low sodium beef stock/broth
	salt and freshly ground pepper to taste

Combine the mushrooms and water in a heat-proof bowl and let stand 30 minutes to soften. Drain the mushrooms, reserving the soaking liquid. Squeeze the mushrooms to remove the excess liquid. If using shiitake mushrooms, cut off and discard the tough stems. Chop the mushrooms and reserve. Line a small strainer with a paper coffee filter and strain the soaking liquid to remove any grit. Set aside.

Place the butter and flour in a ramekin or custard cup. Use your fingers to knead the butter and flour until it forms a paste; this is called a "beurre manie." Heat the olive oil in a Cuisinart® 1 Quart Windsor Pan over medium-high heat. Add the mushrooms and shallots. Cook for 2 to 3 minutes, stirring, until lightly browned. Add the thyme and port. Cook over medium-high heat to reduce until syrupy and the liquid is about 2 tablespoons in volume. Add the reserved mushroom soaking liquid and both the stocks. Cook over high heat to reduce the liquid by about half. This will take about 15 to 20 minutes. When the liquid has reduced by half, lower the heat. Add the butter/flour mixture and simmer while stirring and whisking until the sauce thickens. Taste and adjust seasonings if needed, with salt and freshly ground pepper.

Makes about 1 1/2 cups.

Herbed New Potato & Mushroom Pan Roast with Green Beans

3 tablespoons	extra virgin olive oil, divided
1 pound	new red potatoes (1 inch size), washed
1 pound	new white potatoes (1 inch size), washed
8 ounces	crimini mushrooms, cleaned and halved
2/3 cup	shallots, chopped
1 tablespoon	garlic, thinly sliced
1 teaspoon	salt, divided
2 teaspoons	herbs de Provence*
1 pound	green beans, cleaned, trimmed and cut into 1-inch lengths
	freshly ground black pepper and salt to taste

Heat 2 tablespoons of the olive oil in the Cuisinart® 12-inch Skillet over medium-high heat. When hot and shimmering, add the potatoes and stir to coat. Cook the potatoes for 5 to 10 minutes, until they start to take on a little color. Add the mushrooms and cook about 5 minutes. Stir occasionally and drizzle with the remaining olive oil. Sprinkle the vegetables with the shallots, garlic and 1/2 teaspoon of the salt. Do not stir. Cover loosely and reduce the heat to medium-low. Cook for 30 minutes, stirring every 10 minutes. The vegetables are done when they are tender, but not falling apart. If needed, cook for an additional 10 to 15 minutes.

Add the green beans and stir to combine. Cover loosely and cook for 5 to 10 minutes, or until the beans are tender and cooked to taste. Add the remaining salt and pepper as desired. Serve hot or warm.

Makes 12 servings.

*Other blends, such as Southwestern Herb Mix or an Italian Herb Blend, may be substituted.

Toasted Almond Pear Clafoutis

2	firm ripe pears, peeled, halved and cored
2 tablespoons	fresh lemon juice
3/4 cup	blanched almonds, toasted and sliced
1/2 cup + 2 tbsp.	sugar, divided
3/4 cup	evaporated fat-free milk
1/2 cup	unsalted butter, melted and cooled, divided
3 large	eggs
1 teaspoon	vanilla extract
1/3 cup	cake flour
1/2 teaspoon	baking powder
pinch	salt

Preheat the Cuisinart® Toaster Oven Broiler to 400°F. Butter a 1 1/4-quart baking dish.

Insert the 4-mm slicing disc in the Cuisinart® Prep 11 Plus™ Food Processor. Cut the pear halves in half lengthwise and arrange in the large feed tube. Use medium pressure to slice the pears. Remove the sliced pears to a buttered baking dish and toss with the lemon juice. Spread the pears evenly in the baking dish.

Dry the work bowl with a paper towel and insert the metal blade. Process the almonds and one-half cup of sugar until the nuts are finely ground, about 15 to 20 seconds. Add the evaporated milk, 6 tablespoons of the melted butter, eggs, vanilla, almond extract, flour, baking powder and the salt. Process for 10 seconds. The batter will be smooth and creamy. Do not over blend.

Pour the batter over the pears, drizzle with the melted butter and sprinkle with the remaining sugar. Bake until golden brown and set, about 40 to 45 minutes. Cool on a rack for 15 minutes before serving. To serve, top warm portions with freshly whipped cream.

Makes 8 servings.

New Year's Eve Bash

New Year's Eve is arguably the biggest night of the year for parties when people gather to celebrate the end of the old year and the beginning of the new one.

Come to Our Party

- Type your invitation on a blank label and attach it to a noisemaker. Hand-deliver it to your guests.

A Glittery Gala

- Drape a glittery cloth over the table, creating folds and swirls.
- Use bright, solid-colored plates and dishes.
- String colorful Christmas lights or novelty lights around your party site.
- Place traditional New Year's hats and crowns on the chairs.
- Place white candles of different heights on a large mirror as a centerpiece.
- Light up the night with colorful paper luminaries along your walkway.
- Supply noisemakers and music to enhance the cheer.

NEW YEAR'S FOODS
(Highlighted recipes are included.)

Chili Spiced Nuts

Shrimp Tapas

Seafood Paella with Sausage

Chocolate Truffles

The Best Frozen Margaritas

Seafood Paella with Sausage

I pound	shrimp (16 to 20 count), peeled and deveined
12	sea scallops
12	steamer clams
12	mussels
I	halibut steak, about 1/2 pound
15-ounce	can artichoke hearts, drained on paper towels
2 cups	fat free, low sodium chicken stock, heated
I teaspoon	saffron threads, crumbled
2 tablespoons	extra virgin olive oil, divided
12 ounces	lowfat chicken chorizo or traditional chorizo, sliced 1/2-inch thick
1/2 cup	dry white vermouth or other dry white wine (not Chardonnay)
2 cups	yellow onion, chopped
I tablespoon	garlic, finely chopped
I cup	red or green bell pepper, chopped
2 1/4 cups	basmati or other long grain white rice
2 cups	clam juice, heated
I cup	water
2 to 3 tablespoons	fresh cilantro or parsley, chopped

Use a sharp knife to cut shrimp partially through along the back. Set aside. Remove the tough muscle from the side of the scallops if necessary and slice the scallops in half horizontally. Set aside. Scrub the clams and mussels under cold water and debeard the mussels as necessary, set aside. Skin and bone the halibut steak and cut into 1/2-inch thick slices and set aside. Cut the artichoke hearts in halves or quarters and set aside. Crumble the saffron threads into the hot chicken broth and let it stand.

Heat 1 tablespoon of the olive oil over medium-high heat in a Cuisinart® 5 1/2 Quart Sauté Pan. When hot and shimmering, add the sliced chorizo. Cook sausage until evenly browned, 4 to 5 minutes. Discard any excess grease. Add the vermouth, stirring to loosen the brown bits from the bottom of pan. Cook until the vermouth has reduced by half, 2 to 3 minutes, remove the sausage/wine mixture and set aside.

Reduce the heat to medium-low and add the remaining olive oil to the pan. When the oil is hot, add the onions, garlic and red peppers to the pan. Stir to coat the vegetables with oil. Cover loosely and cook until vegetables are softened but not browned, 5 to 8 minutes. Stir in the rice and cook, stirring frequently, until the rice is opaque, about 5 minutes. Return the sausage/wine mixture to the pan and stir in the chicken stock with saffron, clam juice and the water. Cover and cook for 5 minutes. Stir in the reserved shrimp, scallops, and halibut along with the artichokes and peas. Cover and cook 5 minutes longer. Uncover and arrange the clams and mussels, hinge side down, in the rice mixture. Cover and cook until the clams and mussels are open, the rice is tender and the seafood is cooked, 7 to 10 minutes longer. Discard any unopened clams or mussels. Sprinkle with the cilantro. Spoon the paella onto warmed plates and serve. The paella may be garnished with lemon and tomato wedges.

Makes 8 servings.

Seafood Paella with Sausage — page 90

Shrimp Tapas

I pound	shrimp (16 to 20 count), peeled and deveined
2 tablespoons	extra virgin olive oil
2 cloves	garlic, peeled and minced
I 1/2 tablespoons	parsley, chopped
2 teaspoons	lemon zest, finely chopped
1/3 cup	dry or medium dry sherry
2 tablespoons	fresh lemon juice
I tablespoon	capers, rinsed and drained
	crusty bread for serving, sliced, optional

Rinse the shrimp and pat dry (see recipe tip for instructions on brining, if desired). Toss shrimp with the olive oil, garlic, 1/2 tablespoon of the parsley, and 1 teaspoon of the lemon zest. Heat the Cuisinart® 12-inch Stick-Free Skillet over medium-high heat for several minutes. When hot, add the shrimp, placing them in a single layer, without crowding. Cook, without moving, for 60 to 70 seconds, until they begin to firm up and brown. Turn and cook on the second side for 60 to 70 seconds. Add the sherry and lemon juice. Cook for 1 to 1 1/2 minutes longer, until the shrimp are cooked. Using a slotted spoon or spatula to transfer the shrimp to a serving bowl and toss with the capers, the remaining chopped parsley and lemon zest.

Place the skillet with the remaining juices over high heat and cook to reduce the liquid until thick and syrupy and about 2 tablespoons in volume. Pour the reduced liquid over the shrimp. Serve the shrimp warm or at room temperature as an appetizer. Slice the bread to serve alongside.

Recipe Tip: To make your shrimp juicier and tastier, brine them for a short time before cooking. To do this, combine 2 tablespoons each of salt and sugar with 1 cup boiling water. Stir until the salt and sugar are completely dissolved. Add 10 ice cubes. When the brine is cold, add the shrimp, stir and allow them to stand for 20 to 30 minutes. Drain the shrimp in a colander, pat completely dry using paper towels and continue with the recipe.

Makes 16-20 Shrimp.

The Best Frozen Margaritas

1/4 cup	granulated sugar
1/4 cup	water
6 ounces	golden tequila
3 ounces	**Triple Sec**
4 ounces	fresh lime juice
4 cups	ice cubes

Place sugar and water in a Cuisinart® 1 Quart Windsor Pan. Bring to a boil, then reduce heat and simmer until the sugar is completely dissolved. Transfer to a glass measuring cup and cool to use. This should yield 1/3 cup of simple syrup. (You may make larger batches of the syrup and store it in the refrigerator in a covered jar, if desired.)

Place the simple syrup, tequila, Triple Sec, lime juice and ice cubes in the Cuisinart® SmartPower Premier™ Blender. Place the cover on the blender jar. Press On and blend on High for 30 to 40 seconds until smooth and slushy in texture. Turn the blender Off. Serve immediately in chilled Margarita glasses. If desired, the rims of the glasses may be rubbed with a wedge of lime and dipped in coarse salt. Garnish with a thin slice of lime.

Makes 4 servings.

The Best Frozen Margaritas

Grilled Chicken Breasts with Roasted Red Pepper Coulis — page 97

Chapter 6

Celebrating the Events of Life Together

Birthday Bashes for Both

When you celebrate your birthdays privately, you may choose to plan your special "party of two" with themes geared to a special interest or hobby of his or hers.

His Party

- The night before his birthday, give him a cryptic clue to his birthday celebration by tucking a note into his coat pocket or briefcase, or leave it on his pillow.
- For your dining table cover, choose a masculine patterned sheet or cloth.
- Place a menu written in gold ink on the table.
- Use an ice bucket to cool your wine.
- Place balloons around the room and at his chair.

BIRTHDAY FARE
(Highlighted recipes are included.)

Steamed Artichokes with Olive Tapenade Aioli

Grilled Chicken Breasts with **Roasted Red Pepper Coulis**

Fresh steamed Asparagus

Mocha Chocolate "Chip" Cookies

White wine, champagne or beverage of choice

Steamed Artichokes with Olive Tapenade Aioli

1	**bay leaf**
2 thin	**slices lemon**
3 medium	**artichokes**
1	**lemon, cut in half**

Pour enough water to steam into the Cuisinart® Saucepan. Add the bay leaf and lemon slices to the water and bring to a boil. Reduce the heat to a simmer and cover the saucepan until ready to steam the artichokes. Use a sharp knife to trim 1/2-inch from the tops of the artichokes and trim the stem end flat. Rub the artichoke with lemon immediately after trimming to prevent discoloration. Pull off the tough outer leaves from around the bottom of the artichokes. Rub with lemon. Use sharp kitchen shears to cut off the prickly points of the remaining leaves and rub with lemon. Stand the artichokes in the Steamer. Place the Steamer in the Cuisinart® Saucepan above the simmering water and cover. Steam for 30 to 40 minutes, until the artichokes are tender when tested with the tip of a paring knife in the stem end. Drain well, and serve warm or chilled with a small ramekin of the Olive Tapenade Aioli for dipping.

Olive Tapenade Aioli

1 clove	**garlic, peeled**
12	**Kalamata olives, pitted (drained if in brine)**
1 teaspoon	**fresh lemon juice**
1 teaspoon	**capers, drained**
1/2 teaspoon	**anchovy paste**
1/2 teaspoon	**Dijon-style mustard**
1/2 teaspoon	**herbs de Provence**
1/3 cup	**fat-reduced mayonnaise**

Place the garlic in the work bowl of a Cuisinart® Mini-Prep® Food Processor or Mini-Prep® Plus Food Processor and pulse 5 times to chop. Scrape the work bowl. Add the olives, lemon juice, capers, anchovy paste, mustard and herbs de Provence. Pulse to chop 5 times, then process until a paste is formed, about 30 seconds. Scrape the sides of the work bowl as necessary.

Add the mayonnaise and pulse to mix in. Cover and allow the mixture to stand while the artichokes steam. The Olive Tapenade Aioli may be made a day ahead. Keep refrigerated until ready to use.

Makes 3 servings.

Roasted Red Pepper Coulis

1 tablespoon	unsalted butter
1/3 cup	red onion or shallots, finely chopped
1/3 cup	carrot, finely chopped
1 clove	garlic, peeled and finely chopped
1/2 teaspoon	herbs de Provence
3/4 cup	vermouth
3 large	roasted red peppers, seeds removed, diced*
15-ounce	can diced tomatoes with juices
1/2 cup	fat-free low sodium chicken or vegetable stock or broth
1/2 teaspoon	salt
1/8 teaspoon	freshly ground black pepper

Melt the butter in the Cuisinart® Windsor Pan over medium heat. Add the onion, carrot, garlic and herbs de Provence. Sauté for 1 minute, reduce the heat to low and cover. Cook for 3 to 4 minutes, until the vegetables are tender, but not browned. Add the vermouth. Increase the heat to medium-high and cook uncovered until the liquid is reduced to about one-fourth cup. Add the diced roasted red peppers, the diced tomatoes with their juices and the stock. Bring the mixture to a boil, then reduce the heat to medium-low and simmer for 20 to 25 minutes.

Strain the solids from the liquid, reserving the liquid and returning it to the Windsor Pan. Simmer the liquid over medium heat until it is thickened and reduced by half. Transfer the solids to a Cuisinart® blender or food processor fitted with the metal blade; pulse to chop, then process to purée until smooth. Stir the puréed mixture back into the thickened liquid and keep warm over low heat until ready to serve. The coulis may be used as a sauce for pasta or as a sauce for grilled or poached chicken or seafood.

Makes 3 1/2 cups.

*You may also use roasted red peppers from a jar, drained and seeded. Do not rinse.

Mocha Chocolate Chip Cookies

I cup	pecan halves
2 tablespoons	instant coffee granules
I tablespoon	hot water
2 cups	all-purpose flour
I 1/4 teaspoons	baking soda
1/4 teaspoon	salt
I cup	butter, slightly softened
3/4 cup	light brown sugar, firmly packed
3/4 cup	sugar
I large	egg
I 1/4 teaspoons	vanilla extract
I 1/2 cups	semisweet chocolate chips
	cooking spray

Preheat the oven to 350°F. Place the pecans on a baking sheet and toast until lightly browned, about 3 to 4 minutes. Cool slightly. Fit the Cuisinart® Mini-Prep® Plus Processor with the sharp blade and add the pecans. Pulse on Low speed until coarsely chopped, about 5 times. Set aside. Combine the instant coffee granules and water in a small bowl and reserve. Combine the flour, soda and salt in a small bowl. In a large mixing bowl, use the Cuisinart® SmartPower™ Countup® 9-Speed Electronic Hand Mixer to cream the butter and sugars on speed 2 until light and fluffy, about 1 to 2 minutes. Add the coffee/water mixture, egg and vanilla. Gradually increase to Speed 4 and mix until well blended, about 30 seconds. Add the flour and mix on Speed 2 until combined, about 30 seconds.

Scrape the bowl with a spatula and continue mixing until well blended, about 30 seconds. Add the chocolate chips and pecans. Mix on speed 1 until just combined, about 20 to 30 seconds. Coat baking sheets with the cooking spray. Drop the dough by rounded tablespoonfuls, 2 inches apart, onto the baking sheets. Bake until golden, about 10 to 12 minutes. Cool slightly on the baking sheets and then transfer to a wire rack.

Makes 3 1/2 dozen cookies.

Tip: Cookies store well in the freezer. After baking, cool completely and store in an airtight container in the freezer.

Your Birthday Bash

When your partner is hinting for ways to celebrate your special day, here are some ideas that your spouse can use to express "your birthday is the happiest day of my life." Even the most "domestically challenged" mate can implement these ideas. In this plan, we've designed a perfect day for you. Pass it on!

- If she loves shopping and you don't, map out a shopping spree to include her favorite merchants and accompany her without a whimper, a sigh or a glance at your watch. Include a picnic lunch of finger foods from the recipes you'll find in this celebration guide to hand-feed the lady of the hour.

- Set a lovingly prepared tray to serve her a light spa meal of salad or finger foods in bed.

- After the meal, draw her a hot bath in a tub filled with bubbles and rose petals. Illuminate your bathroom with scented candles. When she's finished her soak, act as a masseur and give her a loving and leisurely massage.

YOUR BIRTHDAY FARE
(Highlighted recipes are included.)

Baby Crab Cakes

Fresh Fruit in bite-sized pieces

Easiest Fudgy Brownies

Baby Crab Cakes

1/2 cup	artichoke hearts, chopped (drain well before chopping)
1/2 cup	saltine cracker crumbs, coarsely ground
1/4 cup	low-fat mayonnaise
1 large	egg, lightly beaten
2 tablespoons	jalapeño pepper, finely chopped
1	shallot, peeled and minced
1 clove	garlic, peeled and minced
2 teaspoons	fresh cilantro or parsley, chopped
1 teaspoon	Dijon-style mustard
1/8 teaspoon	cayenne pepper
8 ounces	lump crabmeat, carefully picked over to remove shell and cartilage
2 tablespoons	unsalted butter
2 tablespoons	extra virgin olive oil
	round tortilla chips
	salsa and guacamole for garnish

In a medium bowl, combine the artichoke hearts, cracker crumbs, mayonnaise, egg, jalapeño pepper, shallot, garlic, cilantro, mustard and cayenne. Stir to combine. Gently fold in the crabmeat. Do not overmix or break up the crab lumps. Shape into 20 mini crab cakes, using a slightly rounded tablespoon as a measure. Place the crab cakes on a baking sheet lined with plastic wrap and refrigerate until firm, at least 1 hour. Heat 1 tablespoon of the butter with 1 tablespoon of the olive oil in the Cuisinart® Skillet over medium-high heat. When bubbly, add 10 crab cakes and cook about 2 to 3 minutes per side, until crispy and browned. Repeat with the remaining crab cakes. To serve, place a crab cake on a chip and garnish with a small dollop of salsa and/or guacamole.

Makes 20 mini crab cakes.

Recipe notes: Crab cakes can be made even smaller. Use a 1/2 tablespoon measure and serve on mini round corn chips. Blue corn chips make a nice accompaniment. Crab cakes can be made larger to serve as a meal. Use about 2 1/2 tablespoons crab mixture to form 8 crab cakes. Serve 2 crab cakes per portion.

Easiest Fudgy Brownies

1/2 cup	unsalted butter
2 1-ounce	squares unsweetened chocolate
1/2 cup	granulated sugar
1/2 cup	light brown sugar
2 large	eggs
1/2 teaspoon	vanilla extract
1/3 cup	all-purpose flour
1/2 teaspoon	salt
1/2 cup	chocolate chips
1/2 cup	walnuts, chopped

Preheat the Cuisinart® Convection Toaster Oven Broiler to 325°F on the Bake setting. Lightly coat an 8-inch baking pan with cooking spray.

Place the butter and unsweetened chocolate in the Cuisinart® 3 Quart Saucepan. Using low heat, melt the butter and chocolate, stirring to combine. Remove from the heat and let it stand 5 minutes. With a wooden spoon, stir in the sugars, eggs and vanilla until the batter is smooth. Add the flour and salt and stir to blend. Fold in the chocolate chips and walnuts and transfer to the prepared pan.

Bake the brownies at 325°F for about 35 minutes. Cool on a rack. When the brownies are completely cool, cut into squares. These are best served while warm.

Makes 16 brownies.

Easy Fudgy Brownies

When Good Things Happen

To flourish as a team, you'll take delight in, as well as give encouragement and support to each other's accomplishments. When job promotions and advancements take place for either of you, a celebration such as a special dinner to show your pride and pleasure is in order. Make it a labor of love with the extra effort you put into arranging fun and unique details for your admiration festivity. Then store away these celebration essentials for the next good news gala.

Promoted and Proud Dinner Party

- Create a "Way to Go!" or "Congratulations!" banner to display for all of your "pat on the back" occasions.
- Cover your table with a shiny gold or silver Mylar (or fabric) cloth.
- Sprinkle gold or silver confetti on the table.
- Use your crystal flutes for a tribute toast of bubbly champagne or sparkling grape juice.
- Your beautiful china, silver and glassware will set the perfect table on which to present your kudos and culinary best.

CONGRATULATIONS! MENU
(Highlighted recipes are included.)

Tossed Green Salad with ripe Tomatoes and Sesame Thai dressing

Caribbean Pork Chops with Fruited Rice

Petite Peas in butter

MiniChip Cheesecakes for 2

Champagne

Caribbean Pork Chops with Fruited Rice

1/2 teaspoon	paprika (sweet or hot, to taste)
1/4 teaspoon	ground cinnamon
1/4 teaspoon	ground ginger
1/4 teaspoon	ground thyme
1/2 teaspoon	salt
1/4 teaspoon	freshly ground black pepper
3	bone-in loin pork chops, 1-inch thick
1 tablespoon	unsalted butter, divided
1/2 tablespoon	extra virgin olive oil
1/3 cup	yellow onion, chopped
1/3 cup	celery, sliced
1 clove	garlic, minced
3/4 cup	basmati rice
2/3 cup	fat-free, low-sodium chicken stock/broth
2/3 cup	water
1 1/2 ounces	dried apricots, cut into slivers (about 1/4-cup)
1/4 cup	dried cranberries

Combine the paprika, cinnamon, ginger, thyme, salt and pepper in a small bowl. Sprinkle on both sides of the chops and rub in. Let the chops stand for 15 to 20 minutes. In the Cuisinart® 12-inch Skillet, melt half the butter with the olive oil over medium-high heat. Holding each chop with tongs, brown the chops for 1 to 2 minutes. Brown each side for 1 1/2 to 2 minutes. Do not move the chops while browning. Transfer the browned chops to a plate. Pour off and discard excess grease.

Reduce the heat to medium-low and add the remaining butter to the pan. When the butter is melted, add the onion, celery and garlic. Sauté until softened, about 2 to 3 minutes. Add the rice and cook, stirring constantly over medium-low heat until the rice is opaque, about 2 to 3 minutes. Add the broth and water and bring to a boil. Stir in the dried fruit, reduce the heat to low, and nestle the reserved pork chops into the rice. Add any accumulated juices from the meat and cover. Simmer over low heat for about 15 to 16 minutes, until the liquid is absorbed and the rice is tender. Remove the pan from heat and let stand, covered, for 5 minutes. Serve hot.

Makes 3 servings.

MiniChip Cheesecakes for 2

	cooking spray
1 1/2 ounces	chocolate sandwich cookies
1/2 tablespoon	unsalted butter, cut in 4 pieces
8 ounces	lowfat cream cheese, cut in 1-inch pieces
1/4 cup	sugar
1 large	egg
2 teaspoons	vanilla extract
4 tablespoons	mini chocolate morsels

Preheat the Cuisinart® Convection Toaster Oven Broiler to 350°F. Lightly coat two 4-inch (1 1/4 cups each) springform pans with cooking spray.

Assemble the Cuisinart® SmartPower™ Duet® Blender/Food Processor with the Food Processor attachment. Insert the metal blade. Place the cookie pieces in the work bowl and pulse 5 times to break up. Add the butter and process 15 to 20 seconds until buttered crumbs are formed. Press the buttered crumbs into the bottoms of the two prepared pans. Bake in the preheated oven for 10 minutes. Place the springform pans in the freezer for 5 to 10 minutes to cool the crumb mixture completely. When cool, wrap each pan in a sheet of aluminum foil so that the foil is at least 1-inch above the side of the pans.

Do not wash the work bowl. Place the cream cheese and sugar in the work bowl. Process 10 seconds. Scrape the bottom and sides of the work bowl and add the egg and vanilla. Process until smooth, about 10 seconds. Scrape the bowl and process for another 5 seconds. Add the mini morsels and pulse 3 times to blend. Divide the batter evenly between the two prepared pans. Place the filled pans in an 11" x 7" baking pan. Add hot water to the baking pan to the depth of 1/2-inch. Bake in the preheated oven for 25 minutes. Remove from the oven, lift out of the hot water carefully and place on a rack. Remove the foil and allow to cool completely. Cover the mini cheesecakes and refrigerate at least 4 hours before serving. If desired, you may double wrap the cheesecakes and freeze for up to 1 month.

Makes 2 servings.

First Anniversary Celebration

Can it be possible that a whole year has gone by since your wedding? And yet, so many new memories have been created in that short time span that will last a lifetime. Turn celebrating your first anniversary into an even more joyful occasion by sharing an intimate meal, watching your wedding video, thumbing through your wedding album and recalling the most important day of your lives. Here are some ways to recreate some of the decorative highlights of your wedding to help your recollections remain crystal clear.

Déjà vu for Two

- Cover your table and chairs with cloths similar to or the same as what was used at your wedding reception.
- Make up a smaller version of your wedding table decor using the same flowers, candles and other accessories.
- Use your best tableware to create ultimate elegance and to even surpass your wedding table setting.
- Place a beautifully framed copy of your wedding invitation and your wedding portrait on the table in a prominent place of honor.
- Play a CD of all of the music featured at your wedding, both from your ceremony and reception.
- Bring out your guest book and read through the names to remember all those important people who shared your special day.
- Play a romantic remembering game of trivia, taking turns with questions, to test each other's recollection of wedding day facts (Any answer, correct or incorrect, earns a kiss.)
- Propose a sentimental and adoring anniversary toast to each other with your wedding goblets.
- Nibble on pieces of your wedding cake, which you've preserved in your freezer for just this day.

LOVER'S FEAST

(Highlighted recipes are included.)

Baby Spinach Salad with Mandarins

Sautéed Shrimp with Rosemary

Gingered Basmati Pilaf with Vegetables

Tarte Tatin with Whipped Crème Fraîche

Sautéed Shrimp with Rosemary

2 cloves	**garlic, peeled**
2 tablespoons	**fresh rosemary leaves**
2/3 cup	**plain breadcrumbs**
1/4 cup	**extra virgin olive oil**
2 tablespoons	**canola oil**
	coarsely ground black pepper
	kosher salt
1 3/4 pounds	**medium-large shrimp (about 30 per pound), shelled and deveined**

In the Cuisinart® Mini-Prep® Plus Processor fitted with the sharp blade, process the garlic on High until minced, about 5 seconds. Add the rosemary leaves and process on High until chopped, about 15 seconds. Scrape the bowl and process an additional 15 seconds. Add the oils and process to combine, about 15 seconds. Place the shrimp in a resealable food storage bag. Add the bread crumbs and toss to evenly coat the shrimp. Add the oil and herbs and seal the bag. Distribute the oil evenly over the shrimp. Refrigerate for 30 minutes to marinate. Heat the Cuisinart® 12-inch Skillet over medium heat. When warm, add the shrimp and sauté for 3 to 4 minutes on each side, or until the shrimp are pink. Turn the shrimp halfway through cooking to brown evenly on both sides. Serve immediately.

Makes 6 servings.

Gingered Basmati Pilaf with Vegetables

1 tablespoon	unsalted butter
3/4 cup	yellow onion, chopped
2 cloves	garlic, peeled and chopped
1 1/4 cups	white basmati rice (you may substitute long grain white rice)
2 slices	fresh ginger, each about 1/8-inch thick
2 1/2 cups	low sodium chicken or vegetable stock
1/2 teaspoon	salt
1 cup	peas, fresh or frozen, thawed
1 cup	julienned carrots (about 4 ounces)
1 tablespoon	Italian parsley, chopped

Melt the butter in the Cuisinart® 3 Quart Saucepan over medium heat. Add the onion and garlic and sauté until tender and translucent, about 2 to 3 minutes. Add the rice. Cook and stir for 3 to 4 minutes until the rice is opaque in appearance. Do not brown the rice. Add the stock and ginger slices and bring to a boil. Reduce the heat to low, cover, and simmer over low heat until the rice is cooked, about 15 to 18 minutes. Stir in the peas and carrots. Cover and turn off the heat. Let the rice stand for 5 minutes. Transfer to a warmed serving bowl and fluff with a fork. Sprinkle with chopped parsley and serve hot.

Makes 8 servings.

Sautéed Shrimp with Rosemary

Tarte Tatin with Whipped Crème Fraîche

1/4 cup	granulated sugar
2 tablespoons	firmly packed brown sugar
6 tablespoons	unsalted butter, cut into 12 pieces
1 teaspoon	vanilla extract
1 1/4 pounds	Golden Delicious apples, peeled, cored and cut into eighths
1 1/4 pounds	Braeburn or Fuji apples, peeled, cored and cut into eighths
2 tablespoons	lemon juice
1 sheet	frozen puff pastry, thawed according to package directions
	flour to dust the counter

Combine the sugars in the Cuisinart® 10-inch Skillet and top with the slices of butter. Heat the sugar and butter over medium heat, but do not stir. Cook until golden brown and bubbly, about 5 to 10 minutes. Add the vanilla extract. Arrange a layer of apple wedges decoratively around the bottom and sides of the pan. Add the remaining apples and sprinkle with lemon juice. Cook the apples over medium heat, without stirring or disturbing, until the juices turn caramel in color and are bubbling, about 1 1/4 to 1 1/2 hours. The apples will reduce in volume.

While the apples are cooking, unfold the thawed puff pastry and dust lightly with flour. Roll out to a 13-inch square. Using the lid for the skillet as a template, cut out a round of puff pastry 12 inches in diameter. Place the pastry on a cookie sheet without sides that has been lined with plastic wrap. Prick the pastry all over with the tines of a fork. Place the pastry in the freezer until ready to use. About 15 minutes before the apples are ready, preheat the oven to 400°F. When the syrup in the apple mixture is a deep caramel color and bubbling, turn off heat. Place the pastry disk over the apple mixture and place the pan in the preheated 400°F oven for about 20 minutes until the pastry is puffed and browned. Remove the tart from the oven and let it stand for at least 15 minutes on a rack to cool.

Just before serving, invert a platter with a rim over the skillet. Using potholders to hold the pan and plate tightly, invert the tart onto the platter. Replace any apples that may stick to the skillet and reshape the tart if needed. Cut the tart into wedges and serve with slightly sweetened whipped crème fraîche or slightly sweetened whipped cream.

Whipped Crème Fraîche

Place 10 ounces of crème fraîche in a medium bowl with 1/4 cup sugar. Use a Cuisinart® SmartPower™ Hand Mixer to whip until light and fluffy.

Makes 4 to 6 servings.

Index

Enjoy Using Cuisinart® Products

Cooking is an adventure, and at the same time, the right tools make it easy. Cuisinart® products are designed to let you perform all the basics, and to exercise your culinary creativity whenever the whim strikes. Cuisinart® products will make a difference in your life. They can handle everything from time-consuming food prep to toasting, brewing, mixing, blending, cooking, grilling, baking, and broiling.

Visit the Cuisinart® website to see the innovative products and recipes that were developed for all the celebrations in your life.

www.cuisinart.ca